This book belongs to:

ETHAN

DK | Penguin Random House

Senior Editor James Mitchem
Senior Designer Elaine Hewson
Edited by Sophia Danielsson-Waters, Hélène Hilton, Violet Peto
Designed by Rachael Hare, Charlotte Milner,
Hannah Moore, Rachael Parfitt, Claire Patané,
Samantha Richiardi, Sadie Thomas
Editorial Assistance Dawn Sirett, Marta Rybarczyk
Design Assistance Eleanor Bates, Pauline Korp, Vic Palastanga
Fact Checker Dr. Kim Bryan
Pre-Production Producer Dragana Puvacic
Senior Producer Amy Knight
Jacket Designer Charlotte Milner
Jacket Coordinator Francesca Young
Creative Technical Support Sonia Charbonnier
Managing Editor Penny Smith
Managing Art Editor Mabel Chan
Publisher Mary Ling
Art Director Jane Bull

First published in Great Britain in 2017 by
Dorling Kindersley Limited
DK, One Embassy Gardens, 8 Viaduct Gardens,
London, SW11 7BW

The authorised representative in the EEA is
Dorling Kindersley Verlag GmbH. Arnulfstr. 124,
80636 Munich, Germany

Copyright © 2017 Dorling Kindersley Limited
A Penguin Random House Company
10 9 8 7
031–297104–Sept/2017

A CIP catalogue record for this book
is available from the British Library.
ISBN: 978-0-2412-7635-8

Printed in Slovakia

For the curious
www.dk.com

MIX
Paper from
responsible sources
FSC™ C018179

This book was made with Forest
Stewardship Council™ certified paper –
one small step in DK's commitment to a
sustainable future. For more information
go to www.dk.com/our-green-pledge

My Encyclopedia of
Very
IMPORTANT
ANIMALS

DK

Contents

All about animals

10 A world of **animals**

12 What is an **animal?**

14 **Land** animals

16 **Aquatic** animals

18 Animals in the **air**

20 What makes a **mammal?**

22 Brilliant **birds**

24 Fantastic **fish**

26 Remarkable **reptiles**

28 All about **amphibians**

30 **Minibeasts**

32 Homely **habitats**

34 Extreme **habitats**

36 Shape **support**

38 Super **skeletons**

40 **Spineless**

42 **Feathered** friends

44 **Mythical** animals

46 Animal **relatives**

48 **Dinosaurs**

50 Finding **fossils**

52 **Endangered** animals

Amazing animals

56 Building **beavers**

58 O is for **orca**

60 Suit of **scales**

62 Heroic **huskies**

64 **Polar** bears

66 Cheeky **chimps**

68 The enormous **elephant**

70 Giant **anteater**

72 Big **cats**

74 In the **bat cave**

76 The **orange ape**

78 The **lion** and the **mouse**

80 Barn **owls**

82 Little and **large**

84 **Penguin** party

86 Golden **eagle**

88 Birds of **paradise**

90 **Hammerhead**

92 Sea **soarers**

94 **Fearsome** fish

96 **Dragons** are real!

98 Crocodile **or** alligator?

100 Sea **turtles**

102 Colourful **chameleons**

104 Rattle**sssssss**snake

106 Clingy **geckos**

108 A **frog's** life

110 Red-eyed **tree frog**

112 Awesome **axolotl**

114 Praying **mantis**

116 **Life** in a **hive**

118 The leaf that **walks**

120 A light in the **dark**

122 The marvellous **monarch**

124 **Buggy** builders

126 **Tarantulas**

128 Octopus **alert**

130 Feeling **crabby**

132 Portuguese **man-of-war**

Animal antics

136 Sticking **together**

138 Unlikely **friends**

140 A penguin **story**

142 Time to **sleep**

144 A winter's **sleep**

146 What's for **dinner?**

148 Food **chain**

150 Taking a **trip**

152 **Hide** and seek

154 Underwater **camouflage**

156 On **defence**

158 **Venom** or **poison**

160 Let's **move!**

162 Using **tools**

164 Sound of the **wild**

166 On **Madagascar**

168 **Darwin's** big trip

170 A **helping** hand

172 Animals and **us**

More very important animals

176 Lots of **spots**

178 Lots of **stripes**

180 Crazy **colours**

182 Going **under**

184 Brilliant **builders**

186 **Divers**

188 Super **soarers**

190 Built for **speed**

192 **Climbers**

194 **Mountain** animals

196 **Desert** dwellers

198 Trip to the **tropics**

200 Wild **woodlands**

202 The **coral reef**

204 **Polar** creatures

206 On the **farm**

208 On **safari**

210 Dazzling **dinos**

212 Perfect **pets**

214 Animal **sounds**

216 What's in a **name?**

218 Animal **words**

220 **Index/Acknowledgements**

All about animals

From little lizards to enormous elephants, Earth is bursting with amazing **animal life**. There are millions of different animals, and new ones are still being discovered. How much do you know about the creatures that share our planet?

A world of animals

Turn the pages to meet animals that are big, small,

Earth's land, seas, and sky are packed with incredible creatures. They can be very different from each other, but they're all **very important!**

scaly, fluffy, spotty, friendly, deadly, and more!

What is an animal?

Whether they **swim**, **fly**, **slither**, or **hop**, all animals are amazing in their own special way. But how do we know what an **animal** is?

Animals and plants

Animals and **plants** are both living things, but in what ways are they different?

Dog

I like to **RUN** and **MOVE** around.

Most animals can choose to **move**, but plants can't.

All animals are VERY IMPORTANT...

Types of animals

Animals come in all sizes, shapes, and colours. Animals that are the same are placed in **species**.

Bear   Snake   Bat   Goose   Monkey

Unlike animals, I get my energy from the **SUN**.

Animals breathe in **OXYGEN** from air or water.

I use my **EYESIGHT** to look for food.

Sunflower

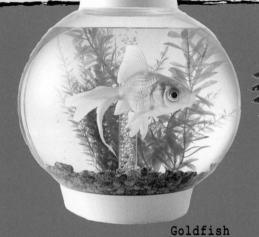

Goldfish

Hawk

Animals need to **eat** to get their energy. Plants don't eat food.

All living things need to **breathe**. Plants take in air, but not the way animals do.

Animals have more developed **senses** such as smell, touch, and sight.

...and people are animals too!

Butterfly

Zebra

Flamingo

Orangutan

Penguin

Cat

Tiger

Frog

Human

13

Land animals

A lot of animals live **on land**.
They don't all look alike, but they are
specially suited to life on the ground.

Snail

Giraffe

Hyena

Mouse

Gorilla

Duck

I spend a lot of time
in rivers but I don't
really swim. I just walk
along the riverbed.

Hippopotamus

Chicken

14

Snake

Spider

Land lovers

Animals that live on land are called **terrestrial animals**. They're found all over the world, in forests, plains, mountains, cities, deserts, and more.

Camel

Dog

Leopard

Cow

Tapir

Pig

I am the *biggest* type of deer.

Hedgehog

Moose

Aquatic animals

Flying fish

Lakes, rivers, oceans, and seas are home to lots of different animals. Creatures that spend all or most of their lives in water are known as **aquatic**.

Jellyfish

Ray

Cardinalfish

Squid

Shark

Eel

Shrimp

Otter

I'm semi-aquatic so I spend half my time in water and half on land.

Sea lion

Dolphin

How do they breathe?

Aquatic animals have different ways of getting oxygen. Fish take in water and oxygen using **gills**. Others, such as turtles and dolphins, come to the surface for air.

Crab

Goldfish

Seahorses

I'm one of the few reptiles that lives in the ocean.

Clownfish

Blue tang

Sea turtle

Octopus

Penguin

Starfish

Sea urchin

17

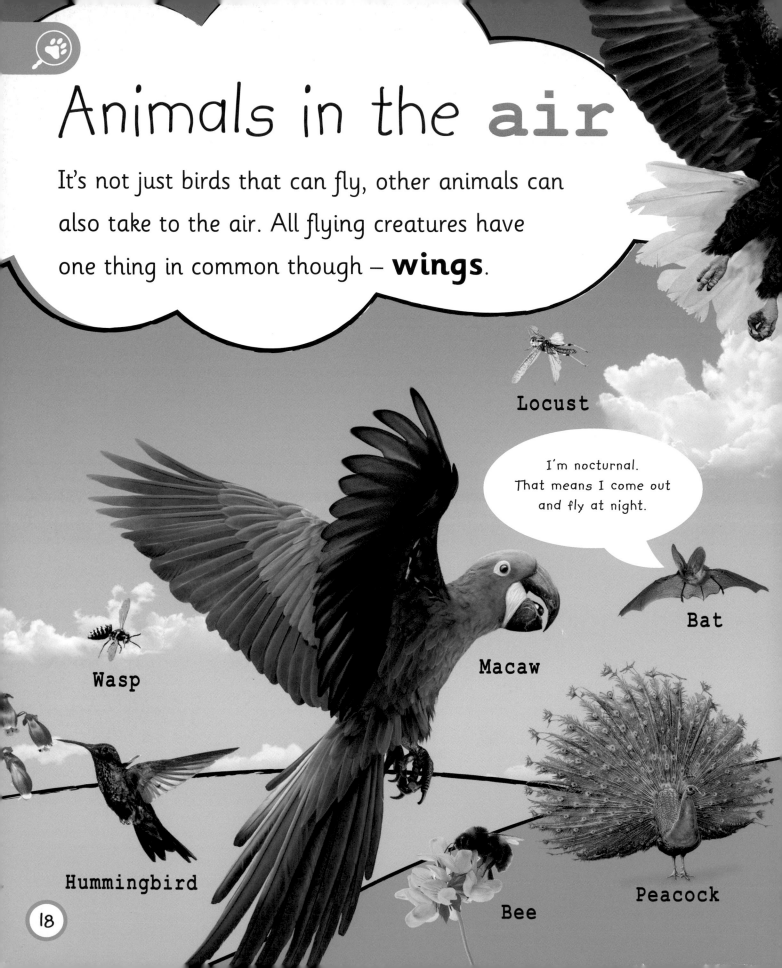

Animals in the **air**

It's not just birds that can fly, other animals can also take to the air. All flying creatures have one thing in common though – **wings**.

Locust

I'm nocturnal. That means I come out and fly at night.

Bat

Wasp

Macaw

Hummingbird

Bee

Peacock

18

Super soarers

Flying animals can move through the air in a **variety** of ways. They can swoop, soar, dive, glide, and hover. Hummingbirds can even fly backwards!

Toucan

Budgerigar

Eagle

Puffin

Owl

Pigeon

I can fly, but not very far.

Butterfly

Ladybird

Cockerel

Flamingo

Moth

19

What makes a **mammal?**

Mammals are a **group** of animals. They come in many shapes and sizes, but they do have a few things in common.

Am I really like a POLAR BEAR?

Did you know that PEOPLE are MAMMALS?

Born as babies
Whether they live on land or in water, almost all mammals are born instead of hatching from eggs like birds. Every baby mammal drinks **milk**.

Warm-blooded
All mammals are **warm-blooded**. This means that they keep a constant body temperature whether they're in a hot jungle or in the freezing snow.

Elephants are one of the only mammals that can't jump.

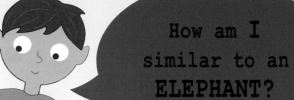

How am I similar to an ELEPHANT?

Don't forget us! We're mammals too!

Bats are the only mammal that can fly.

People say I'M like a TIGER!

Elephant leg bones

Human lower leg bones

Similar skeletons

Mammals can look very different, but they all have a bony **skeleton** on the inside. You have a backbone, and so do elephants. You don't have a trunk though!

Furry friends

Some mammals are more fluffy than others, but almost all of them have **hair**. The hairs on your head are quite like the hairs on a tiger, only they're not stripy!

21

Brilliant birds

One thing people think of when they think of birds is **flight**, but there are birds that can also run and swim with ease. Birds can do it all!

Pheasant

Emu

Owl

Not all birds can fly. Some of us stay on the ground and run fast!

World of birds

Birds are one of the most varied animal groups on Earth. There are more than **10,000** species, and they can look and behave very differently from each other.

Duck

Vulture

Hawk

Parrot

Woodpecker

An extra long beak helps
hummingbirds reach into
flowers for delicious nectar.

Hummingbird

What links them?

Although birds can look and act very
differently, there are a few things they
all have in common.

Birds have feathers that
keep them warm and dry.

All baby birds hatch from eggs.

Birds have beaks to help them
eat and clean themselves.

Puffin

A long tongue and a sharp
beak helps a puffin carry
lots of fish in its mouth at
once. What a mouthful!

Fantastic fish

Whether they're in rivers, lakes, ponds, or seas, fish have lots of special features that helps them **live underwater**.

Angelfish

Seahorse

Butterfly fish

> I look a little different, but I'm still part of the fish family.

A group of fish is called a **school**. When fish swim together, it makes it harder for predators to pick out just one.

Gills

Instead of **breathing** with lungs like people, most fish use gills to get oxygen from water.

Gills allow fish to breathe.

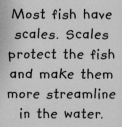

Most fish have scales. Scales protect the fish and make them more streamline in the water.

Fishy family

There are more than **33,000** different types of fish, and they come in a whole range of shapes, sizes, and colours.

Scales

Opening to gills

Fin

I have venomous spines to protect myself from predators.

Lionfish

Bull shark

Plaice

Fins

Fins help fish stay the right way up in the water. Fish also use their fins to steer as they **swim**.

Swordfish

Cold-blooded

Most fish are cold-blooded, so their bodies stay the same **temperature** as the water.

25

Remarkable reptiles

Reptiles are a group of animals with a special type of protection. Their bodies are covered in waterproof plates called **scales**.

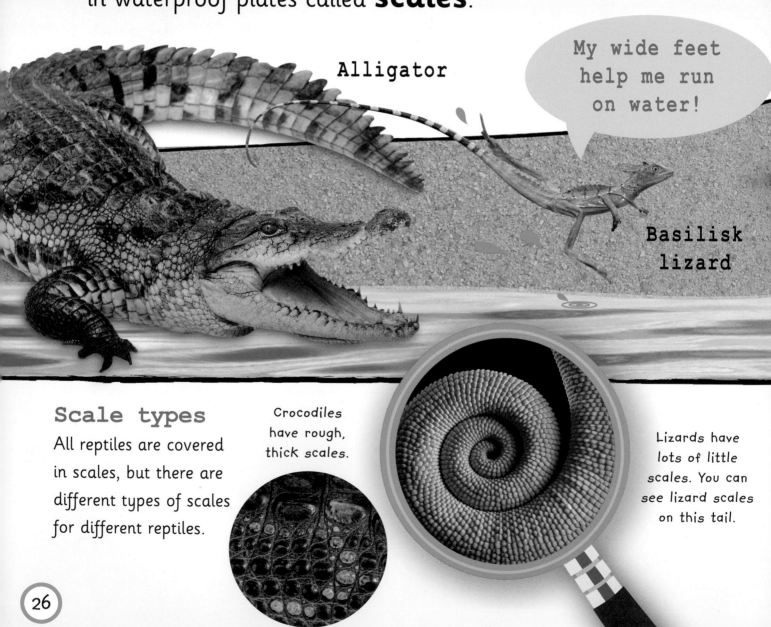

Alligator

My wide feet help me run on water!

Basilisk lizard

Scale types

All reptiles are covered in scales, but there are different types of scales for different reptiles.

Crocodiles have rough, thick scales.

Lizards have lots of little scales. You can see lizard scales on this tail.

Seeking the Sun

Unlike mammals, reptiles are **cold-blooded**. This means they need to sit out in the sun to warm up.

Nelson's milk snake

> I live a long and slow life. I can live to be more than **100 YEARS OLD.**

Shedding

All reptiles will shed their skin from time to time to get rid of old scales. When snakes do this, it all comes off at once!

Giant tortoise

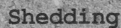

Some reptiles live in water.

Turtle

Snakes have smooth scales that overlap each other.

A tortoise's skin has small scales and its shell has large ones.

Little hatchlings

Most reptiles hatch from eggs. A lot of reptiles lay their eggs underground to keep them safe.

All about amphibians

Amphibians are a group of animals with a special ability: most are perfectly able to live on **land** and in **water** as adults.

Frog

Frogspawn

Tadpoles

Froglet

I'm growing up fast!

Newt

Life cycles

Amphibians lay eggs in water. The tadpoles that hatch from the eggs **change** as they grow, eventually growing legs and coming onto land.

Land and water

Most amphibians spend part of their lives on **land** and part in **water**. But there are some that prefer one more than the other.

Tree frog

I have STICKY PADS on my feet that are excellent for CLIMBING.

Toad

Salamander

I look like a worm, but I'm an amphibian!

Caecilian

Cold-blooded

Amphibians are **cold-blooded** and cannot control their body temperature. They get hotter or colder depending on the weather and their surroundings.

Slippery skin

Most amphibians have smooth, moist skin with no scales or hair. But what's most special about their skin is that it allows them to **absorb oxygen**.

Minibeasts

Dragonfly

Fly

Creepy-crawlies such as flies, ants, spiders, and crabs, all belong to a large group of animals called **arthropods**.

Moth

A world of bugs

Arthropods are the most successful animals on Earth. There are **more of them** than other animals, and they've been around for millions of years.

Bee

Butterfly

Ladybird

Types of arthropod

Earth's thousands of different arthropods are split into different groups. Here are the main ones.

INSECTS

Bees, ants, flies, and beetles are insects. Insects have **six legs** and three body sections. Most of them have wings.

 **Ants**

A good way to find out which group an arthropod belongs to is to count its legs.

Centipedes and millipedes belong to a group of arthropods called "Myriapoda".

Centipede

Scorpion

Woodlouse

Crab

Spider

Tarantula

Lobster

ARACHNIDS

Arachnids are animals such as spiders and scorpions. They have **eight legs**, and don't have wings.

Harvestman

CRUSTACEANS

Animals such as crabs and lobsters are called crustaceans. They usually have **10 or more legs**.

A lobster's front legs are called claws.

Homely habitats

Animals live in lots of different places around the world. These places are called **habitats**, and each one has animals that are specially suited to live there.

Rainforests

These rainy tropical forests are rich with plants and animals. They're very **hot** and humid, and almost half the world's animal and plant species live there.

There is lots of tasty fruit to eat in the rainforest.

Wetlands

Wetlands are places that link land with water. They can be very **swampy** and are usually filled with all kinds of animals, such as fish, birds, reptiles, and amphibians.

I'm glad it's wet where I live. If it wasn't I might dry out!

Forests

While rainforests are **hot and humid**, there are other forests that usually have warm summers and cold winters.

This forest is full of tall trees for me to climb.

Grasslands

Many of the animals that live in grasslands travel in herds. They are usually on the move looking for new **grass** to graze on.

I'm known as the king of the jungle, but I'm the top hunter of the grasslands.

Other habitats

Animals are very adaptable, and can be found in almost every corner of the Earth. Here are a few other places that animals call **home**.

 Cities

 Caves

 Rivers

 Coral reefs

33

Extreme habitats

There are some places where animals live that are hard for people to visit. But the animals in these places are **specially suited** to thrive there.

Oceans

The world's oceans are filled with **all sorts** of animals, including fish, mammals, and more. Most of them live near the surface as the depths are dark and cold.

I'm an octopus. You can find us in most of the world's oceans.

Deserts

Places where it hardly ever rains are called deserts. Since there's very **little water**, it's tough to survive, and not many animals live there.

I'm a thorny lizard. It's very hot and dry where I live.

Mountains

There isn't much soil on mountains so there aren't many **plants** for animals to eat. It can also get very cold there.

Mountain goats like me are great at climbing.

Polar regions

The top and bottom of our planet are the polar regions (the Arctic and Antarctica). They're **cold** and **dry**, and it's hard to find food there.

I'm a walrus. The fat in my body helps me stay warm in the cold.

Different deserts

Most deserts are sandy or rocky, and extremely hot. But Antarctica, which is the **coldest place on Earth**, is a desert too.

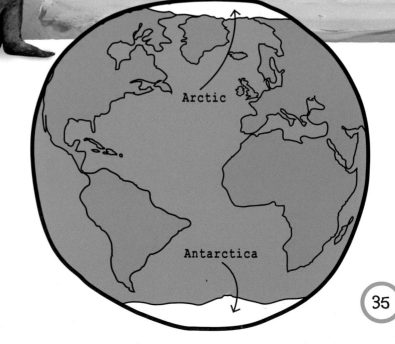

Arctic

Antarctica

Shape support

Animals come in lots of **shapes** and **sizes**. But how do animals keep their shape, stay upright, and move?

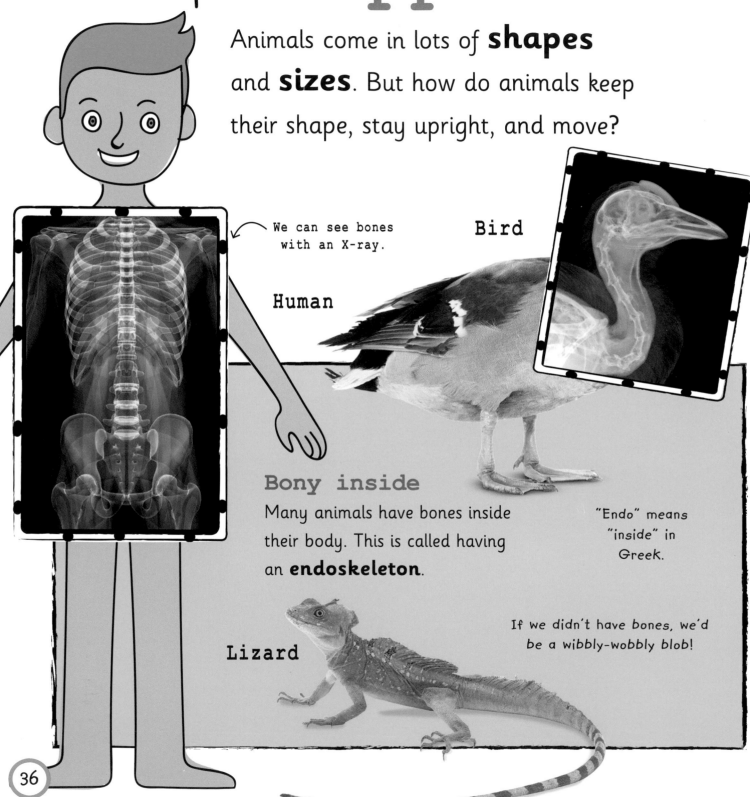

We can see bones with an X-ray.

Bird

Human

Bony inside

Many animals have bones inside their body. This is called having an **endoskeleton**.

"Endo" means "inside" in Greek.

Lizard

If we didn't have bones, we'd be a wibbly-wobbly blob!

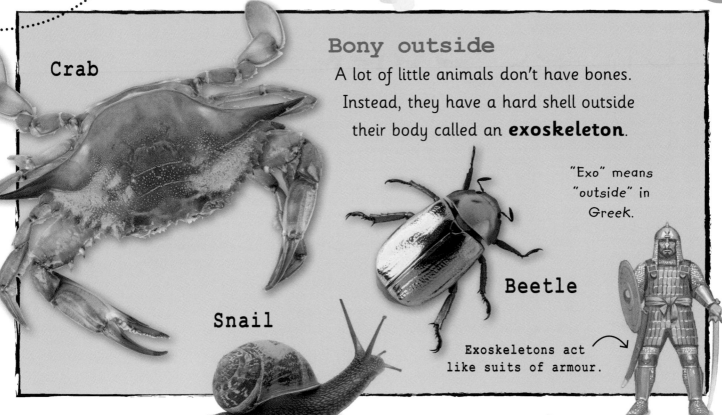

Crab

Bony outside

A lot of little animals don't have bones. Instead, they have a hard shell outside their body called an **exoskeleton**.

"Exo" means "outside" in Greek.

Beetle

Snail

Exoskeletons act like suits of armour.

No bones!

Some animals don't have bones on the inside **or** outside. Instead, they have liquid insides, and their muscles help them move.

Jellyfish

Anemone

You can *see* my rings of muscles. They surround my liquid insides.

Earthworm

Jellyfish use their muscles to push water in and out of their bodies. This makes them move.

Super skeletons

Animals have different types of skeletons based on their **needs**. Some are strong, whereas others can be light or flexible.

There are no bones in my trunk.

Elephant

Where's the trunk?

Elephants are best known for their **trunks**, but if you look at their skeleton you won't find one! That's because their trunks are made of muscles and no bones.

Bird

Birds' bones are hollow because they need to be light enough to fly.

Here are some other animal skeletons.

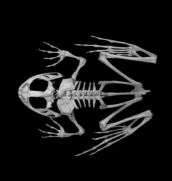

Frog
In order to jump long distances, frogs have long bones in their toes and hind limbs.

Snake
The reason snakes are so bendy is because they've got so many bones in their back.

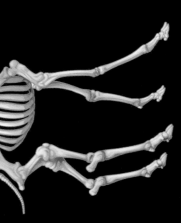

Giraffe
Surprisingly, a giraffe's neck has seven bones, which is the same amount as a human's.

Tortoise
Tortoises have bones on both the inside and outside of their bodies.

Spineless

Most of Earth's animals are **invertebrates**, which means they don't have a backbone. Where can you find invertebrates? Almost everywhere!

Nine out of every ten animals on Earth are invertebrates!

In the water

Rivers and **seas** are full of invertebrates. That includes snippy lobsters with a hard outer shell, and soft, squishy jellyfish.

Sea urchin

Lobster

Jellyfish

On the ground

Take a look beneath you. There are millions of invertebrates living on or below the **soil**, such as worms, woodlice, and lots of different beetles.

Worm

I may be spineless, but I'm still fierce!

Stag beetle

Woodlouse

What are backbones?

A backbone acts like a big beam in a skeleton to **support** an animal's body. Invertebrates don't have internal skeletons. Instead, they have a hard outer shell or a body filled with liquid.

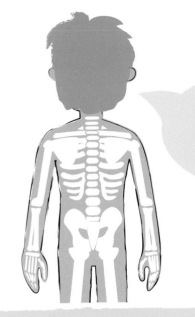

People are not invertebrates. We have backbones.

On plants

If you look at **plants** and **trees**, many of them are crawling with creatures. Ants, stick insects, and spiders are all invertebrates.

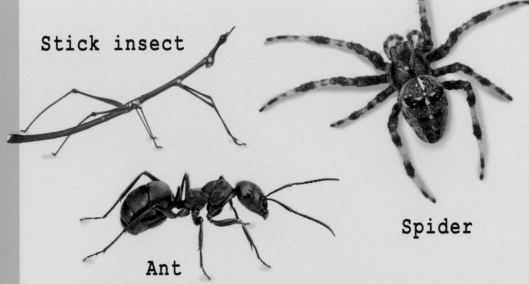

Stick insect

Ant

Spider

In the sky

Other than birds and bats, most animals that **fly** are invertebrates. This includes bees, wasps, flies, butterflies, moths, and mosquitoes.

Wasp

Mosquito

Butterfly

41

Feathered friends

Birds can look very different from each other, but they all have **wings**, **feathers**, and **beaks**, and they all **lay eggs**. They can't all fly though.

Bone

Down feather

Wing feather

Contour feather

Hollow bones

Most birds have bones full of little air pockets. This makes birds **light** enough to fly. The skeleton of most birds weighs less than all their feathers.

Feathers

Birds have different feathers for different jobs, such as flying or staying warm. Feathers are made from **keratin** – the same material as our fingernails.

Eggs

Baby birds hatch from eggs. Eggs can be different **shapes, sizes,** and **colours**. Birds usually lay their eggs in a nest before they hatch.

Beaks

Birds' beaks are different shapes depending on what the bird **eats**. Hooked beaks are good for picking up seeds, and long beaks are better for catching fish.

43

Mythical animals

Tales of magical lands full of strange animals have been passed down for generations. Did these curious creatures ever exist, or were they a case of **imagination** and mistaken identity?

Narwhal

Unicorns

According to legend, these white horses with a **single horn** had magical healing powers. Years ago, people used to sell narwhal tusks and pretend they were unicorn horns.

Unicorn

People have been telling stories and drawing picture of unicorns for thousands of years.

Kraken

Kraken

Kraken

From Norwegian mythology, the kraken is an enormous sea monster with long **tentacles**. Was this mysterious beast really just a giant squid?

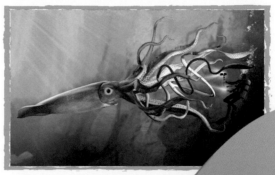

Giant squid

Dragons

These flying reptiles feature in stories across many cultures. Some describe them as enemies, while others say they bring **good luck**. It is possible that ancient people mistook dinosaur fossils for dragon remains.

Dinosaur fossil

Dragon

45

Animal relatives

The Earth is very old, and many animals have **changed** over time. But some animals that lived long ago look a lot like the animals still here today.

THEN

Mammoths lived at the same time as early humans.

Mammoths were like giant **elephants** with bigger tusks and shaggy coats. Their coats helped them stay warm during the Ice Age, when the Earth was freezing cold.

NOW

THEN

WOW that's big!

The **archelon** was a massive **sea turtle**. It was about as long as a giraffe is tall!

The leatherback turtle is the closest living relative of the archelon.

THEN

The **megalodon** was a deadly shark three times bigger than a **great white shark** – the deadliest shark alive today.

A megalodon's tooth was as big as a human hand!

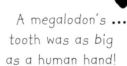

THEN

Smilodons look a lot like big **tigers** or **jaguars** with long teeth, but they aren't related to any cats still around today.

Smilodons had incredibly long, sharp teeth.

Dinosaurs

Long ago, millions of years before people were around, these mighty **reptiles** used to walk the Earth.

Ankylosaurus was covered in bony plates that protected its body.

Ankylosaurus
(Ank-ill-oh-SORE-us)

Stegosaurus
(STEG-oh-SORE-us)

The word "dinosaur" means

Clues from the past
Fossils are the remains of animals and plants from long ago found in rock and ice. Scientists study fossils to learn about dinosaurs.

Fossilized dinosaur skeleton

Time periods

The dinosaurs existed across such a long period of time that most of the different types would **never have met**.

Archaeopteryx
(ar-kee-OP-ter-ix)

Tyrannosaurus rex
(TIE-ran-oh-SORE-us rex)

T. rex was a fierce predator with very sharp teeth.

"terrible lizard"!

Where did they go?

Around 65 millions years ago, a giant meterorite crashed into the Earth. Only small animals survived, which is one of the reasons the dinosaurs disappeared.

Oh no, look what's coming!

Finding fossils

There are animals that once roamed the Earth, but no longer exist. We call these animals **extinct**. Everything we know about them, we know from fossils.

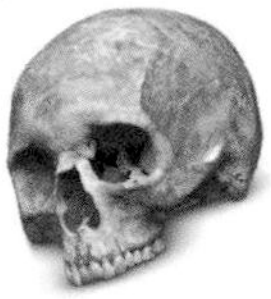

What is a fossil?

Fossils are the **remains** of animals or plants from long ago that have been preserved in the Earth. Studying fossils helps us **learn about the past**.

Turtle fossil

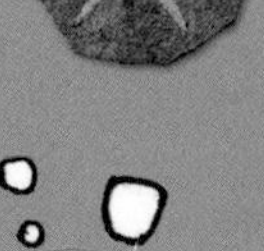

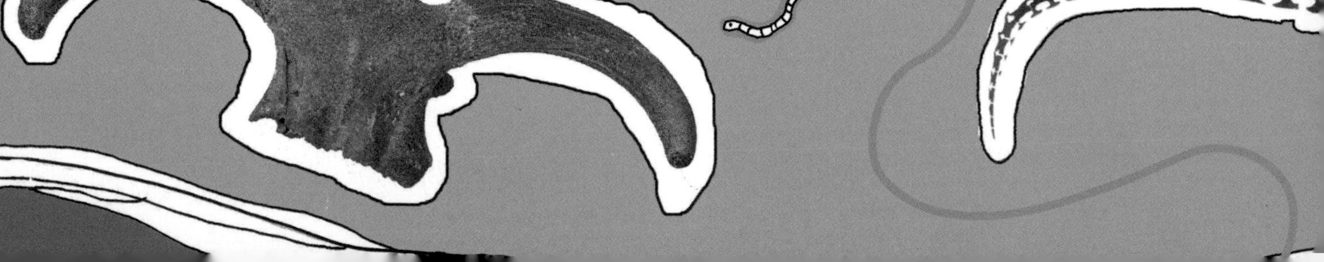

Where do they come from?

Living things only turn into fossils if they are quickly **buried** after they die. The most common fossils are shells that quickly sink into the soft seabed.

Fossils can *be* preserved in rock, amber, or ice.

Bones, teeth, eggs, footprints, and even poo can *become* fossils!

Fish fossil

Dinosaur fossils

It takes millions of years for things to become fossils. They are very rare.

Endangered animals

Sadly, some animals are endangered, which means there **aren't many** of them left in the wild. But there are people working hard to change this.

Good news
Since whale hunting was banned, the number of **humpback whales** has gone up and they are no longer endangered!

The cause
Animals mostly become endangered because of people **hunting** them or causing **damage** to their habitats.

Thank you for helping to keep us safe!

ENDANGERED: Bluefin tuna

VULNERABLE: Dugong

CRITICAL: Hawksbill turtle

CRITICAL

These are examples of animals in danger of becoming **extinct**. Unless something is done, there may not be any left soon.

Mountain gorilla

Northern bald ibis

Sumatran tiger

ENDANGERED

These are some animals that could become extinct if we are not careful. Their numbers in the wild are already **very low**.

African wild dog

Galapagos penguin

New Zealand sea lion

Red panda

VULNERABLE

Polar bear

These are examples of vulnerable animals. Their numbers in the wild are low enough to start being a **concern**.

African elephant

Marine iguana

Amazing animals

Whether they're feathered or furry, smooth or scaly, or friendly or fierce, everyone has their **favourite animals**. Turn the pages to learn fun facts about lots of incredible creatures. You might even discover a new favourite while you're at it!

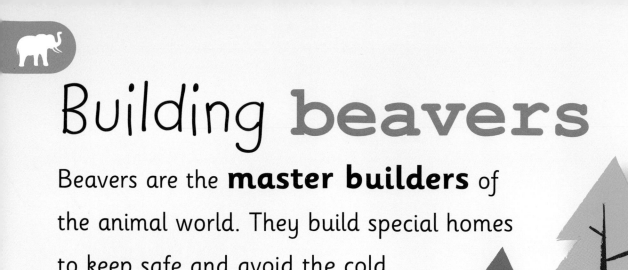

Building beavers

Beavers are the **master builders** of the animal world. They build special homes to keep safe and avoid the cold.

Dam

Home sweet home

Beavers use branches, mud, and stones to build **dams** on rivers. Dams stop the water flow, creating a perfect place for a beaver's home.

A toothy tool

When we build, we use tools and big machines, but all beavers have to work with are their very **sharp teeth**!

Beavers build the entrance to their home underwater so that predators can't get in.

Lodge

A beaver's home is called a "lodge".

Underwater entrance

Sharp teeth help beavers cut trees.

Beavers have flat tails that help them swim. They also use their tails to slap the water and warn each other of danger.

O is for orca

Also known as **killer whales**, these intelligent giants live in oceans around the world. They may look like big fish, but they're actually mammals.

Dorsal fin helps with stability.

Although they're called whales, orcas are a type of dolphin.

Big tail fin helps them swim through water.

A thick layer of fat called blubber helps them stay warm.

Orcas can squirt water from their blowholes high into the air.

Part of the pod

Orcas live in family groups called **pods**. They use a series of clicks and whistle sounds to communicate with each other.

Big hunters

These giants are one of the deadliest hunters in the ocean and they aren't afraid of anything. They work as a team to catch their prey.

I'd better go. Orcas like to eat seals!

Suit of scales

Is that a walking pine cone or a spiky anteater? No, it's a super-scaly **pangolin**! It's the only mammal in the world with scales.

A baby pangolin clings to its mother's tail until it is strong enough to walk on its own.

When pangolins are born, their scales are soft. They harden up over time.

A pangolin's tongue can be longer than its body.

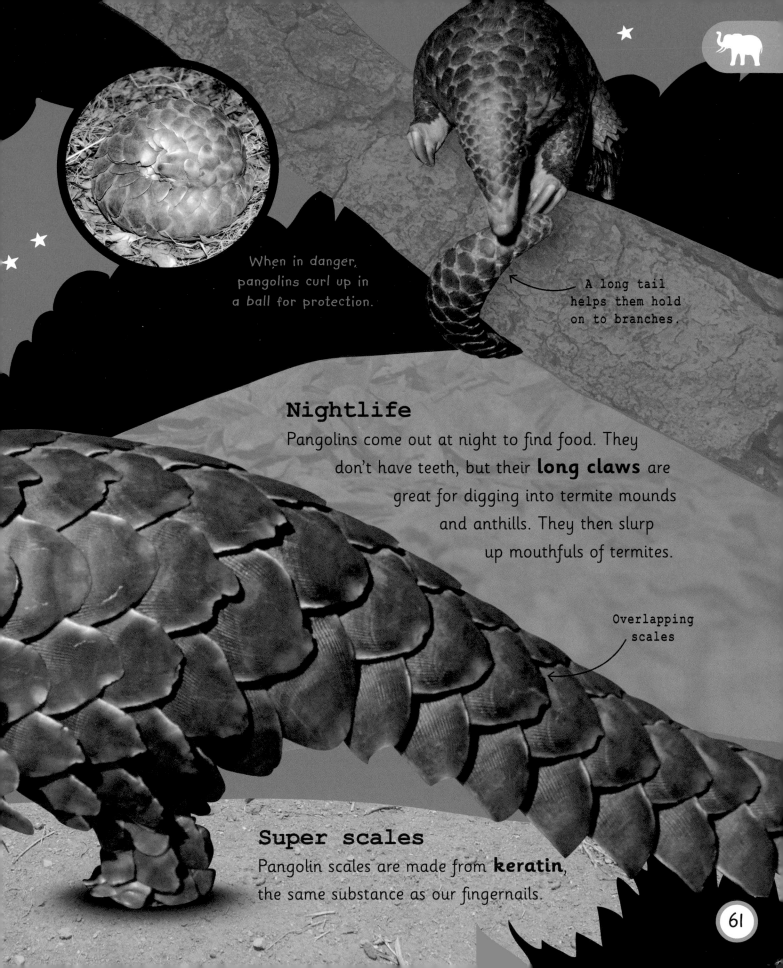

When in danger, pangolins curl up in a ball for protection.

A long tail helps them hold on to branches.

Nightlife

Pangolins come out at night to find food. They don't have teeth, but their **long claws** are great for digging into termite mounds and anthills. They then slurp up mouthfuls of termites.

Overlapping scales

Super scales

Pangolin scales are made from **keratin**, the same substance as our fingernails.

Heroic huskies

This true story of heroic dogs that risked it all to save a town is a great example of why dogs are one of our greatest **animal companions**.

In the winter of 1925, people in the town of Nome, Alaska, became very ill. The town didn't have any **medicine** and the weather was too **bad** for boats, planes, or horses to bring any.

The town's only hope was a group of brave volunteers and their **huskies**, who would work in relays and deliver the medicine by sled.

The weather was **SO COLD** that the rivers and lakes were **FROZEN** over.

N

Nome

Nenana

The group set off on a dangerous journey 1,085km (674 miles) long, through freezing winds and subzero temperatures.

The journey took five long days and nights...

Tired but triumphant, they arrived at Nome with the medicine and the ill people were saved! The brave dogs and people became heroes.

Today, there is a statue in Central Park, New York, to remember the brave dogs and sled drivers.

Polar bears

These big, tough bears live in the Arctic where it is very, very **cold**. Polar bears are specially adapted to survive in the freezing conditions.

I'm one of the biggest and strongest land animals in the world. I'm not afraid of the cold!

Super swimmers

Polar bears are good swimmers. They dive into **icy water** to get between different areas of the sea ice.

Baby polar bears are called cubs.

LOOK OUT! Those bears look HUNGRY!

Arctic

White coat keeps them hidden while hunting on the ice.

64

Cheeky chimps

Chimpanzees belong to a group of animals called apes, and are our closest living animal relatives. No other animals on Earth are more like **people** than chimps.

Chimpanzee hand

That's handy
Chimps have **opposable thumbs** just like humans. This means they can grip objects and use tools.

Chimps are clever, and can

Family and friends
Chimps live in groups called **troops**. Members of the troop groom each other as a way to get clean and make friends who will support them.

Chimps have long arms that are great for swinging from branch to branch.

Baby chimp

use tools, such as sticks.

Chimps usually walk on all fours using their knuckles.

Chimps can communicate using facial expressions and sounds.

67

The enormous elephant

As the largest land animal on earth, everything about elephants is **big** – especially their appetite!

Feeding machines

Elephants need to eat and drink a **lot**. They can drink enough water to fill a whole bathtub every day!

Asian elephants have small ears.

African elephants have large ears.

One elephant can weigh as much as three cars!

Eating a lot of food means that elephants make a lot of poo!

Types of elephant

African elephants have large ears that look like the map of **Africa**. Asian elephants have smaller ears that look a little like **India**.

India

Africa

African elephant

Elephants use their trunks to breathe, gather food and move it to their mouths, and spray water.

Giant anteater

These hungry creatures use their big noses to sniff out ant and termite **nests**. Finding a nest is good news for an anteater, but bad news for their prey!

Back for more

Anteaters are careful not to destroy any nests they find. Instead, they wait for the nests to be **repaired** so they can go back for more!

Grrr! Leave our nest alone. We've only just repaired it.

Anteaters don't have teeth. They swallow their meals whole!

Finding food

Once anteaters find a nest to raid, they use their sharp claws to tear holes in it, then poke in their **long tongues** and feast. They have to eat quickly or they will get bitten and stung by ants!

Saliva and little spines cover an anteater's tongue, helping prey stick to it.

An anteater's tongue can stick out more than 60cm (2ft).

Anteaters can eat up to 35,000 ants and termites every day!

Big cats

Our cute and fluffy pet cats come from the same family as lions, tigers, and other big cats. Can you spot the similarities?

Family of cats

All cats eat meat, so they are adapted to **hunt**. They all have a strong bite to grab their prey, pointy teeth to rip through meat, and very sharp claws.

Leopard

Cheetahs are slender and tall. They are the fastest land animal on Earth.

Domestic cat

Cougar

Snow leopard

Cheetah

Only grown-up male lions have manes.

Tigers are the biggest of all the big cats.

Lion

Tiger

Black panthers are really jaguars or leopards that are a different colour.

Black panther

Jaguar

Many bats hang upside down from branches and rocks while they sleep.

Greater horseshoe bats

In the **bat cave**

★

Although some mammals can glide, bats are the only ones that can **fly**. Not only that, they have a special way of finding their way around in the dark.

> Bat colonies can have more than 20 MILLION bats in them!

Some bats are sociable and gather in

Vampire bats feed on the blood of cows and other animals!

Vampire bat

Blind as a bat

Bats sleep during the day, and many of them live in dark caves. Most bats don't have good **eyesight**, but make up for it with great hearing and something called echolocation.

Long-eared bat

There are more than 1,300 different types of bat.

large colonies.

Squeak Squeak

Echolocation

Bats use sound to find their way around. They make high squeaks that travel through the air and bounce off trees and obstacles. The bats use the **echoes** to "see".

The orange ape

Unlike other apes, most orangutans live alone. But mother and baby are always together.

The biggest animal living high up in the trees is the amazing **orangutan**.

Terrific tree-dweller

Orangutans live in **forests** on two islands in Asia, called Borneo and Sumatra. These apes have long arms that help them swing through trees, and only the heavy males venture down to the forest floor.

Some male orangutans grow cheek pads and beards as they get older.

Orangutans love to eat fruit, especially the stinky durian.

Cheek pad

Durian fruit

The lion and the mouse

One day while out for a walk, a little **mouse** came across a huge **lion** blocking her path.

> If I'm very quiet, maybe the lion won't wake up.

The mouse had no choice but to climb over the sleeping lion. Suddenly, the lion **woke up** and grabbed the mouse by her tail!

"Tell me, Little Mouse, why shouldn't I eat you?" said the lion.

"Because if you don't, I promise to help you one day." said the mouse.

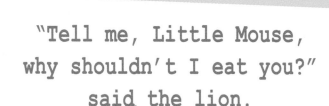

The lion found this so funny, he decided to **let the mouse go**. "A tiny mouse like you would never be able to help a great big lion like me!" he laughed.

A few weeks later, the mouse heard a loud roar. It sounded like the lion was in **trouble**.

ROAR! ROAR!

The lion was caught in a **hunter's net**! The mouse knew exactly what to do.

She started to nibble through the ropes of the net, chewing and chewing until the lion was **free**. The lion was amazed!

"I was wrong about you, Mouse! You may be small, but you're capable of great things."

Barn owl

Owls are one of the master **hunters** of the bird world. Follow the pictures and see how a little egg turns into such a skilled hunter.

Like all birds, owls **hatch** from eggs. When they're ready to come out they use a special tooth on their beak to break the shell.

After a few weeks the owls become fluffy **fledglings**. First, they develop down feathers to keep warm, then a little while later they develop flight feathers.

Despite their name, barn owls don't all live in barns. But they do like to nest indoors.

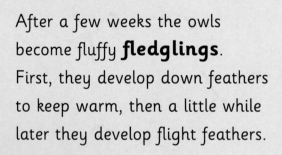

Soon, owls develop enough size, strength, and balance to be able to leap from their nests and **take flight**.

Special skills

Owls' bodies are specially adapted to help them find and catch their prey.

Ears

Owls are better at hearing than almost any animal in the world. Their ears are at different heights, which allows them to pinpoint their prey in the dark.

Most owls hoot, but we barn owls make a screeching sound.

Eyes

Owls have big eyes that help them see better in low light.

Feathers

Special feathers allow owls to fly silently. This means they can sneak up on their prey and catch it by surprise.

Talons

Sharp talons (claws) let owls easily catch small mammals such as mice, voles, and shrews.

Little and large

All bird species lay eggs and have feathers, wings, and beaks. But they can be very **different**. There's no better example of this than looking at a hummingbird and an ostrich.

Hummingbirds

Hummingbirds are one of the world's smallest birds. They can be as small as a bee. Hummingbirds are amazing fliers, and can beat their wings **80 times** a second!

Long beaks help hummingbirds reach the nectar inside flowers.

Hummingbirds can fly backwards, hover in mid-air, and even fly upside down.

Hummingbird egg

Chicken egg

Ostriches
While hummingbirds are tiny, ostriches are bigger than people! They **can't fly**, but they have long legs, and can run very fast.

Ostrich egg

Actual sizes

A newly born ostrich is already much *bigger* than a fully grown hummingbird.

An ostrich is strong enough to carry a man. But they don't like it!

Penguin party

These funny birds mostly live in very **cold** places, but they have a few tricks to help them stay warm.

Keeping warm

A penguin's feathers are packed closely together. This **traps air** and stops the penguin getting too cold.

When it gets very cold, emperor penguins huddle together for warmth.

Types of penguin

There are 17 different species of penguin. Little penguins, the smallest species, are only a little bit taller than this book!

Emperor Penguin

King Penguin

84

Getting around

Penguins **can't fly**, but they are excellent swimmers that move effortlessly in water.

Penguins feast on fish, krill, and squid.

Wings help penguins "fly" underwater.

Gentoo
Penguin

Adelie
Penguin

Rockhopper
Penguin

Little
Penguin

Golden eagle

When people think of a master hunter, their first thought might be a lion, tiger, or shark. But nobody should forget about the **master of the skies**.

Fully outstretched, a golden eagle's wingspan is longer than a person.

Built to hunt

With their soaring speed, powerful talons (claws), and incredible eyesight, golden eagles are amazing **hunters**. One of the only things they need to be afraid of is other eagles.

Strong, hooked beak

Golden eagles are named for the golden feathers on their crown.

86

Stalking the skies

Golden eagles seek out their prey from above, then **dive** towards it, tucking their wings into their bodies to help them reach incredible speeds.

Golden eagles hunt alone or in pairs.

Razor sharp talons

Birds, rabbits, foxes, and even deer are easy prey for an eagle.

Birds of paradise

Many birds are bright and colourful, but male birds of paradise are the real show-stealers. Their bold **colours** and puffy feathers are a sight to behold!

King of Saxony bird of paradise

Where do they live?

This group of beautiful birds is mostly found in the tropical **rainforests** of New Guinea, a large island in the Pacific Ocean, near Australia.

Raggiana bird of paradise

Wilson's bird of paradise

Stephanie's astrapia

Red bird of paradise

Only the male birds of paradise are this brightly-coloured.

Twelve wired bird of paradise

Male

Female

Dancing display

Male birds of paradise will do anything they can to **impress** the females, such as dancing, hanging upside down, and making funny noises.

Look at the funny dance that the male victoria's riflebird does!

The dance begins...

The male pulls some impressive moves...

...at last the female arrives!

Hammerhead

This shark may look a little **strange**, but its wide head and unusual eye position mean it has excellent **vision**.

Hammerheads live in warm, tropical waters.

I swing my head around near the *seabed* to find food.

Super sight

Having an eye on each side of their head means that hammerhead sharks can see in almost **all directions**. But they have a blind spot above and below their heads.

It's easy to see how hammerhead sharks get their name!

Eye on each side of its head.

Watch out, rays!

Hammerheads swim close to the seabed, moving their head from side to side. **Sensors** on their head help them find rays hidden under the sand. When they find a ray they pin it down with their head and eat it.

Rays like me are the hammerhead shark's favourite food.

Sea soarers

Manta rays are **giants** of the sea. As they gracefully flap their huge fins, it looks like they're **flying** through the water.

Manta rays sometimes leap out of the sea.

Gentle giants

Fin tip to fin tip, manta rays are wider than a **giraffe is tall!** Something that big might look scary, but manta rays aren't dangerous to most animals. They only eat tiny creatures called plankton.

Manta rays swim near the sea's

Small stingers

Manta rays are just one member of the ray family. Other rays are smaller and often have painful stings.

Bluespotted ribbontail ray

Blue spots warn other animals to stay away.

Pit stop!

A manta ray stops to get **cleaned** (a little like at a car wash). It makes a signal, and cleaner fish rush to eat tiny parasites on the ray's body and mouth.

Rays are a type of fish. There are around 500 types of ray.

Rays are closely related to sharks.

surface, in warm open waters.

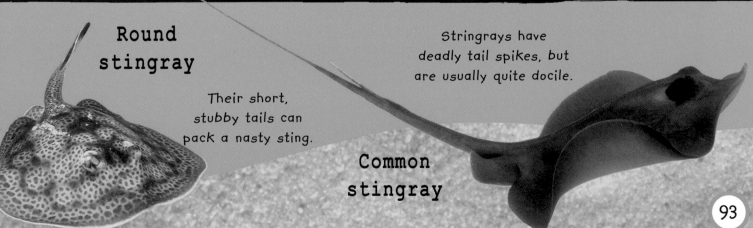

Round stingray

Their short, stubby tails can pack a nasty sting.

Stringrays have deadly tail spikes, but are usually quite docile.

Common stingray

Fearsome fish

Piranhas are toothy fish that live in the rivers of South America. This **red-bellied piranha** is the fiercest type.

A gruesome grin

Piranhas have **sharp teeth** and **strong jaws**. Some only eat fruits and nuts, but red-bellied piranhas eat insects, bigger animals, and even each other!

Piranha means "tooth fish".

A group of red-bellied piranhas can eat an

Feeding frenzy

If red-bellied piranhas are starving they can **swarm** on weak prey that enters the water and eat **it right down to the bone!**

We mostly swim in groups to stay safe from the birds and caimans that hunt us. Caimans are relatives of alligators.

animal down to the bone in one minute!

Big eyes help piranhas see in murky water.

Are they deadly?

Piranhas have a **scary** reputation, but most don't eat meat. Even red-bellied piranhas only become aggressive when they are starving or have no room to move.

Dragons are real!

It may not breathe fire or be able to fly, but that doesn't stop the **komodo dragon** from being the world's biggest, scariest lizard.

Komodo dragons only live on islands in Indonesia, a country in Asia.

Buffalo

Komodo dragons can hunt really big animals, such as deer and buffalo.

The lizard king

Komodo dragons are the kings of the reptile world. They're so scary that the only thing a komodo dragon is afraid of is a **bigger** komodo dragon!

Deadly spit

One of the most amazing things about a komodo dragon is its **tongue**. It uses it to "smell" its prey from afar — and can sort of "taste" its food before eating it!

Watch out! A Komodo dragon's bite is venomous!

Survival instinct

Only the biggest and toughest komodo dragons dare to explore the islands. Little ones stay safe by living in **trees** until they're about 4 years old.

Crocodiles and alligators may look similar, but they're not the same. However, one thing these hostile hunters have in common is that there's no escaping their powerful jaws!

I'm a crocodile.

Usually **paler** in colour.

Crocodile or

Usually **darker** in colour.

Have shorter, **wide**, "U" shaped snouts.

Alligator

Have longer, **narrow**, "**V**" shaped snouts.

Their bottom **teeth stay visible** when their mouths are closed.

They live in **freshwater** and **saltwater**.

Crocodile

alligator?

Their bottom **teeth are hidden** when their mouths are closed.

They live in **freshwater**.

I'm an alligator.

Which is deadlier?
Both crocodiles and alligators are dangerous hunters, but crocodiles are more aggressive, have a stronger bite, and are usually bigger than alligators.

Sea turtles

Like tortoises, turtles are **reptiles**.
But unlike tortoises, sea turtles live most
of their life in the sea, and only come
onto land to lay their eggs.

Turtles are
cold-blooded
reptiles.

Baby turtles have to
move quickly unless they
want to be an easy meal for
crabs and birds.

Time to hatch

During nesting season, female turtles
swim ashore at night and dig a hole
for **their eggs**. Then they swim back
to sea and leave the eggs behind.

1

A female turtle crawls across the beach to
find a safe spot to dig a nest for her eggs.

Turtle travels

Mummy sea turtles look for the **perfect beach** to lay their eggs. Most of them travel back to the beach where they were born!

I can hold my breath underwater for up to seven hours!

2 After about six weeks, the eggs hatch and the babies crawl out.

3 The turtles dig themselves out of the nest and rush to the safety of the sea.

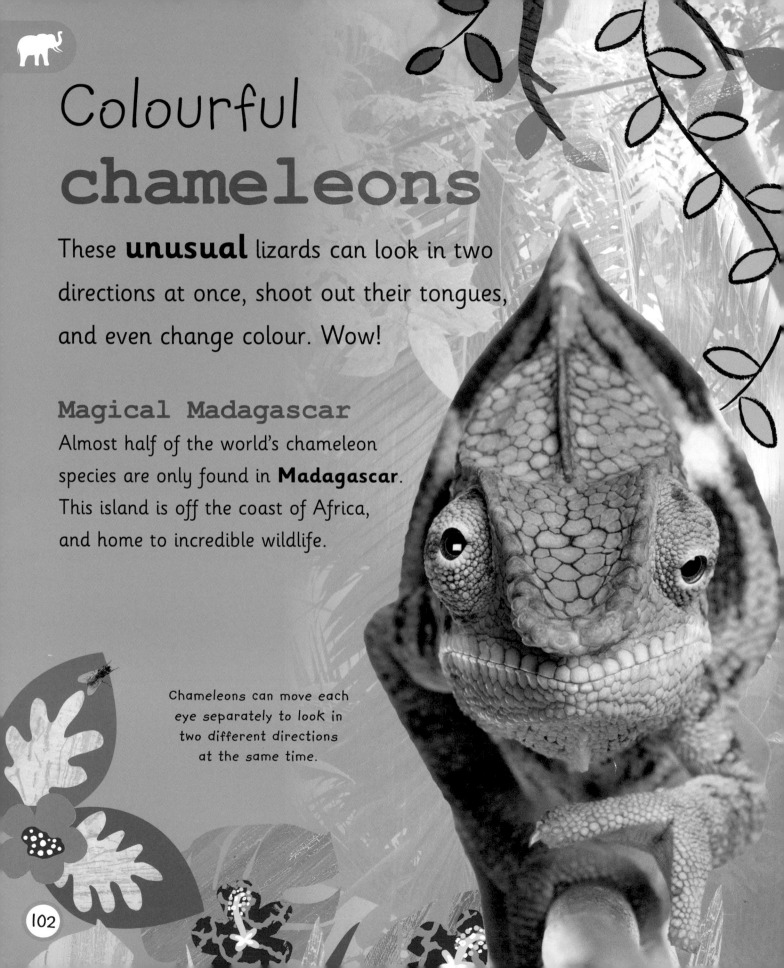

Colourful chameleons

These **unusual** lizards can look in two directions at once, shoot out their tongues, and even change colour. Wow!

Magical Madagascar

Almost half of the world's chameleon species are only found in **Madagascar**. This island is off the coast of Africa, and home to incredible wildlife.

Chameleons can move each eye separately to look in two different directions at the same time.

Sticky traps

The tip of a chameleon's tongue is sticky. A chameleon **shoots** out its tongue to catch insects, such as crickets and flies.

What a tasty looking cricket!

Some chameleons can change into almost any colour of the rainbow.

Cool colours

The most amazing thing about chameleons is their ability to **change colour**. They do this depending on their temperature and their mood.

Long tails help them grip branches.

Rattle**sss**sssnakes

These sneaky snakes have a shaking "rattle" at the end of their tails to warn enemies to **stay away**. Enemies that don't, might receive a very nasty bite!

Rattlesnakes usually move very slowly,

Forked tongue can be used to "smell" where prey is.

A rattlesnake's guide to   hunting

1 Sssssseek out

Snakes don't have ears like we do, so they can't listen for prey. But they can feel **vibrations** around them, and even detect nearby heat. They use these special skills to track down food.

but if they're disturbed, they're lightning fast!

Noisy rattle

Rattlesnakes have rings made of keratin at the end of their tails. They shake them to make a noise and warn off enemies.

Rattlesnakes feed on small animals, such as mice.

rattle
rattle

in three   ssssteps!

2 Sssssstrike

Once a rattlesnake finds its prey, it uses its fangs to inject the animal with deadly **venom**. The venom either kills the prey or stuns it so it can't get away.

3 Ssssssswallow

Finally, the rattlesnake opens its mouth wide and **swallows** the prey whole!

Clingy geckos

Geckos are little lizards with a very **sticky skill**. Can you run up walls or hang upside down from the ceiling? Geckos can!

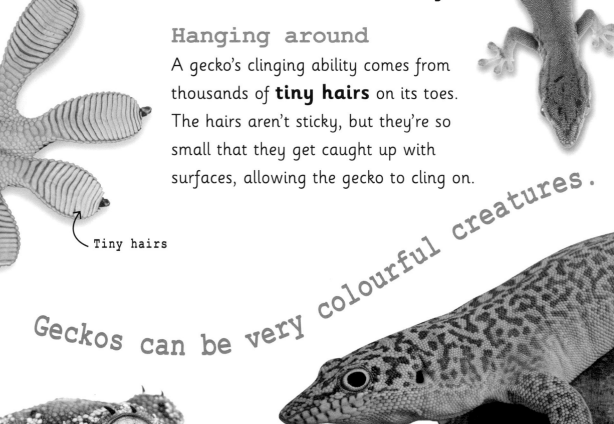

Electric blue gecko

Hanging around

A gecko's clinging ability comes from thousands of **tiny hairs** on its toes. The hairs aren't sticky, but they're so small that they get caught up with surfaces, allowing the gecko to cling on.

Tiny hairs

Geckos can be very colourful creatures.

Northern spiny-tailed gecko

Geckos don't have eyelids, so they lick their eyes to keep them clean!

Slip up!

Geckos can stick to almost anything, but they have trouble with **teflon**™ – the material that non-stick frying pans are made from. Luckily for geckos, teflon isn't found in the wild!

Oh no! I'm slipping.

Ulber's gecko

Can you see the camouflaged gecko on the bark?

Green gecko

Palm gecko

Some types can even change colour!

Yucatan banded gecko

Standing's day gecko

A frog's life

Frogs are amphibians, which means they can live on land and in water. Frogs start off as eggs, and go through several **changes** before becoming adults.

1

A female frog lays lots of eggs, called frogspawn, in water.

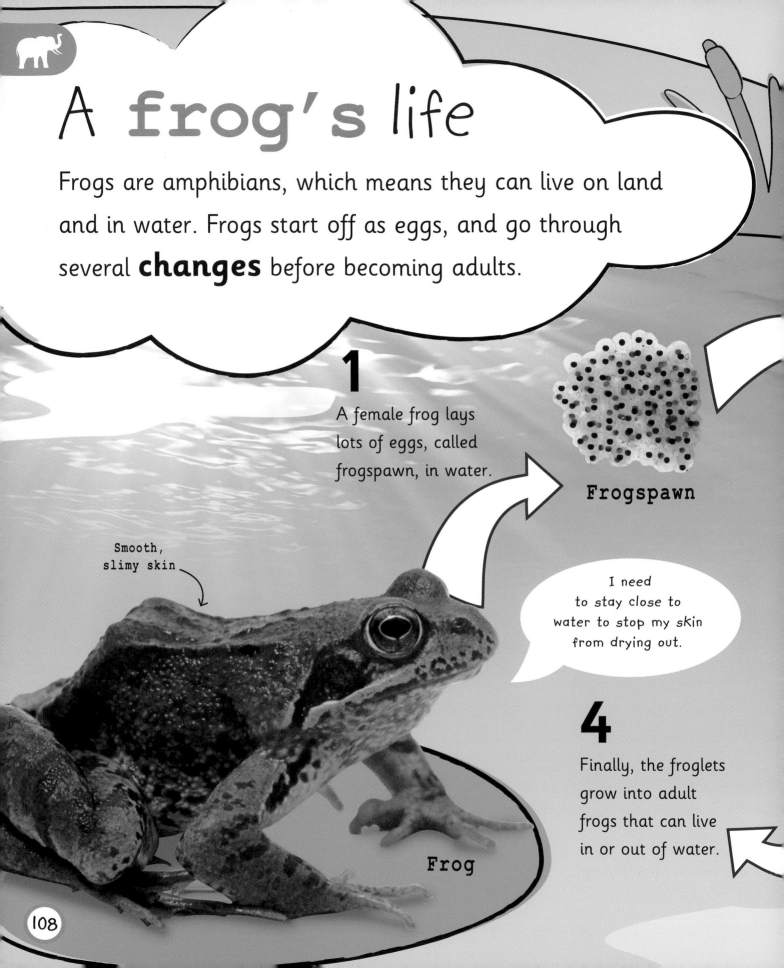

Frogspawn

Smooth, slimy skin

I need to stay close to water to stop my skin from drying out.

4

Finally, the froglets grow into adult frogs that can live in or out of water.

Frog

Frog or toad?

The best way to tell the difference between frogs and toads is to look at their skin. Frogs have **smooth**, **wet** skin, and toads have **bumpy**, **dry**, skin.

I don't mind dry skin, so I can live further away from water than a frog.

2

Tadpoles hatch from the eggs. They have tails and live in water.

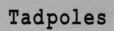

Tadpoles

Dry, bumpy skin

Toad

3

Over time, tadpoles grow into froglets, which have stubby legs and a small tail.

Froglet

Toad life-cycle

Toads have a similar life-cycle to frogs, but they lay their eggs in a line, rather than in a bunch like frogs.

Red-eyed tree frog

These friendly-looking frogs are found in hot tropical forests. They're **brightly coloured**, but also very good at hiding.

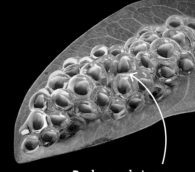

Red-eyed tree frogs lay their eggs on leaves.

Hide and seek

Red-eyed tree frogs are only active at night. During the day they tuck their arms and legs close to their bodies and **shut their eyes** so their bright colours don't give their location away.

> We hide in trees to stay safe.

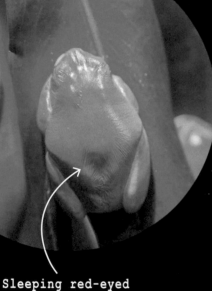

Sleeping red-eyed tree frog

Sticky pads on their toes help them grip leaves and branches.

Escape tactics
These clever creatures are masters of the **quick getaway**. If a predator comes close, they quickly open their bright red eyes, surprising their enemies just long enough for them to hop to safety.

Bright colours
There are lots of frogs that live in trees. They are some of the most colourful animals in the world.

Fringe tree frog

Dyeing poison frog

Red poison dart frog

> Look at me. I'm teeny tiny!

Awesome
axolotl

Most amphibians look different as adults than they do when they're born (think of frogs and tadpoles). But axolotls **don't change** – they just get bigger.

Baby axolotl

Amazing ability

While lots of amphibians can **grow new limbs**, axolotls go one step further. They can also regrow their spines, organs, and even their brains.

Axolotls don't go on land like other amphibians. They enjoy the water too much.

Most axolotls grow to be about my size.

Axolotl is pronounced "AXE-oh-LOT-ul".

Wild adult axolotl

Axolotl means "water dog".

Strange salamanders

These amphibians are very **unusual**. They don't change as they grow, they regrow body parts and they can only be found in one place in the wild.

Soft, thin skin

Feathery gills used to breathe

No eyelids

Big mouth

Young axolotl

Praying mantis

These curious creatures have nifty ninja moves. They **pounce** on their prey so **quickly** that it's hard to see them doing it!

Orchid mantis

Living traps

Mantises are the **deadly hunters** of the insect world. They blend into their surroundings and then strike in an instant to take down prey.

On the hunt

A mantis uses its **huge eyes** to spot its prey. Then it finds a hiding spot and waits for insects, spiders, mice, frogs, or lizards, to get close enough to ambush.

1 A mantis stands perfectly still until a fly gets **close enough** for it to pounce.

Praying mantis

Dead leaf mantis

Mantises are very good at camouflage.

To spot prey, a mantis can turn its head around and look behind it.

It's my dinner time!

2 The mantis grabs the fly with its spiky forelegs and uses its strong jaws to finish off its meal.

Life in a hive

Honeybees live together in groups called colonies. They have homes called **hives**, which are very busy places full of of bees buzzing around.

Drones are the only males in the hive. They help the queen make eggs, and never leave the hive.

Drone

The boss of the hive is the **queen bee**. She is the only bee that can lay eggs. Worker bees clean and feed her.

Worker bees are the busiest of all! They build the hive and help protect it from any attackers.

The queen bee is by far the largest bee in the colony.

Worker bees also make and store **honey**. They gather nectar and do a special dance to tell other bees where to find more.

Honeybees you see outside the hive are all workers. They carry **pollen** from flower to flower, which helps plants spread seeds.

When it gets cold, bees cluster together to keep warm.

Nectar is left in the little holes of a **honeycomb**, and it becomes thick and gooey honey. When it's ready, the worker bees store it – it's their food for the winter.

The leaf that **walks**

Is that leaf moving? No, it's actually a sneaky **leaf insect** using clever camouflage to avoid being eaten!

Leaf insects sway when they walk to look like leaves blowing in the wind.

More leaf pretenders

Leaf insects aren't the only animals that look like leaves. Here are some other animals it would be **hard to spot** in a forest.

Asian leaf frog

This frog spends most of its time on the **forest floor**, so looking like dead, brown leaves helps it stay hidden.

Clever camouflage

The reason leaf insects look so much **like leaves** is to make it hard for birds to spot them. Leaf insects eat leaves, so they might need to be careful not to take bites out of each other by mistake!

Leaf-tailed gecko

This master of disguise looks just like tree **bark** and **rotten leaves**. Many have notches on their tails that look like bite marks.

Leaf katydid

Being **shaped like a leaf** helps this katydid hide from the many predators that might eat it.

A light in the **dark**

What would you do if you were out in the dark and couldn't find any light? Well, if you were a **firefly**, you could just make your own!

Lightning bugs

Fireflies contain special **chemicals** in their bodies. When the chemicals mix together it generates a quick flash of glowing light.

There are around 2,000 types of firefly,

Great glowers

Although fireflies are the most well-known animals that **create light**, other animals do this too. Most of them live in dark caves or in the ocean.

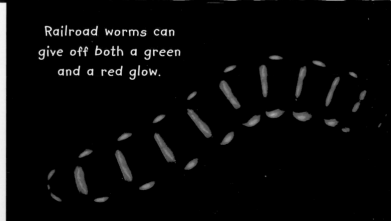

Railroad worms can give off both a green and a red glow.

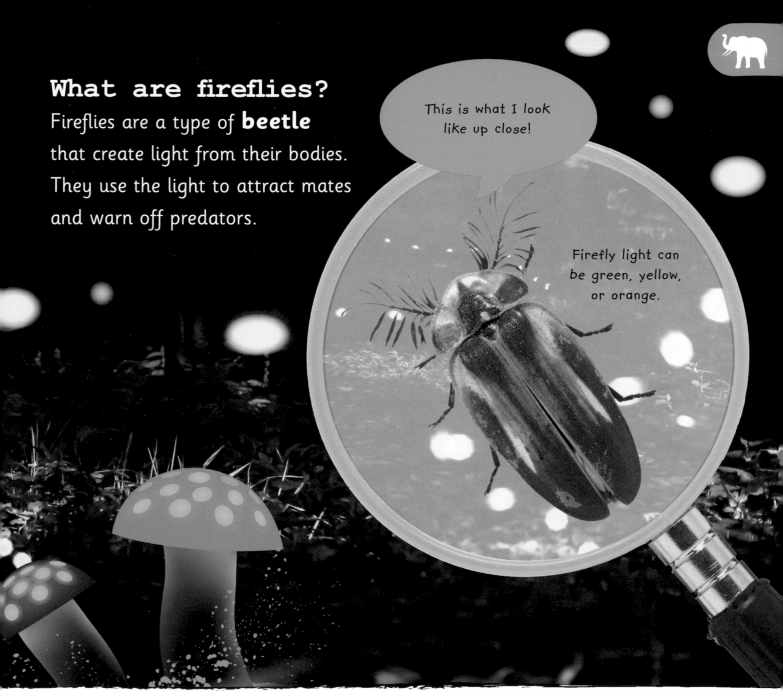

What are fireflies?

Fireflies are a type of **beetle** that create light from their bodies. They use the light to attract mates and warn off predators.

This is what I look like up close!

Firefly light can be green, yellow, or orange.

but not all of them can produce light.

Spectacular firefly squids can light up different parts of their bodies in a series of patterns. They can use their light to communicate with each other.

The marvellous
monarch

Every year, some monarch butterflies go on an amazing **journey** to escape the winter cold. But the butterflies who come home are not the ones who left.

Living longer

Most monarchs only live for two months, but the ones born just before winter on the east coast of North America live for **seven months**. They need this time to make the journey.

> We navigate using the Sun.

Migration route ↴

1

When it gets cold, the monarchs set off from Canada and head south towards Mexico, where it is warmer.

2

It's a long journey that can take two months. When the butterflies arrive they have a nice long sleep.

Only monarchs that live on the east coast of North America make this journey.

The way that the baby monarchs make it home is a big mystery.

Young monarchs often return to the very same tree the journey started from.

3
When spring arrives, the monarchs wake up and head back north to feed. On the way they lay eggs and die.

4
The eggs hatch, and it's up to the babies (or even their babies) to finish the long journey home.

Buggy *builders*

Termites are tiny insects, but they're also master builders. They work together to build huge earth mounds full of tunnels.

Massive mounds

Termites live in huge groups, called **colonies**. A colony lives together in an earth mound. Termites are tiny, but their mounds can be as tall as a giraffe!

Hot air rises up and leaves through a vent.

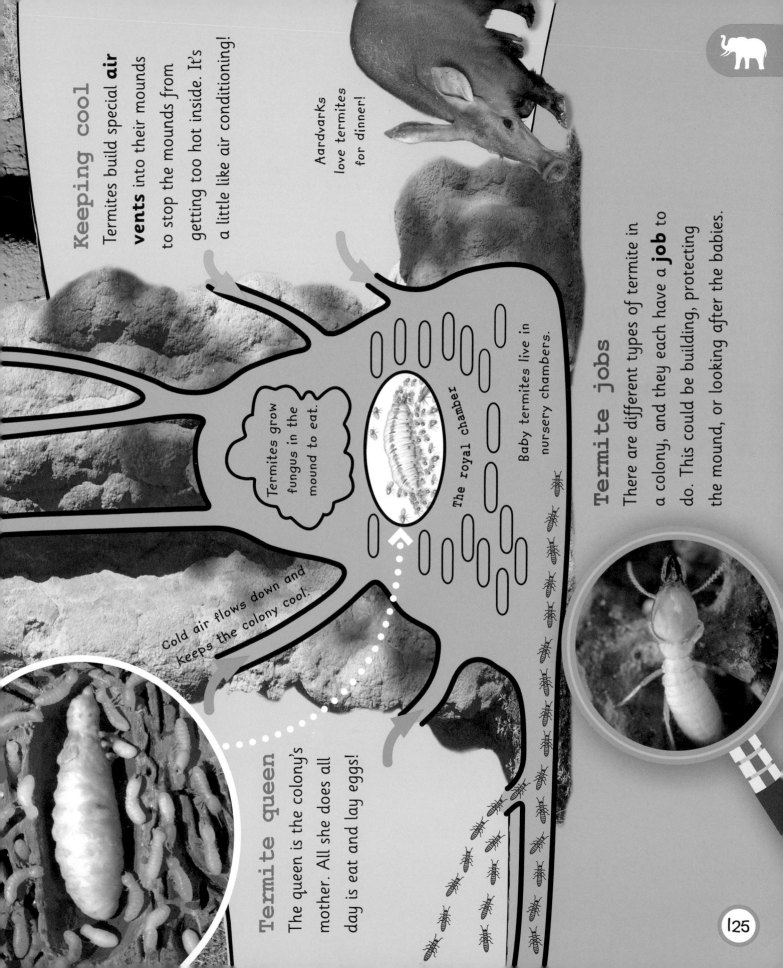

Keeping cool

Termites build special **air vents** into their mounds to stop the mounds from getting too hot inside. It's a little like air conditioning!

Aardvarks love termites for dinner!

Termites grow fungus in the mound to eat.

The royal chamber

Baby termites live in nursery chambers.

Cold air flows down and keeps the colony cool.

Termite queen

The queen is the colony's mother. All she does all day is eat and lay eggs!

Termite jobs

There are different types of termite in a colony, and they each have a **job** to do. This could be building, protecting the mound, or looking after the babies.

Tarantulas

Tarantulas are **big spiders** with fuzzy legs and bristly bodies. Unlike many other spiders, they don't spin webs, and most of them burrow under the ground.

Are they deadly?

No – tarantulas are hairy, not scary! They carry **venom** in their fangs, but it usually isn't strong enough to hurt people.

Fang

The **Mexican red-kneed tarantula** is generally docile. However, if it feels threatened, it flicks spiky hairs at attackers, which can sting them and get in their eyes.

The massive **goliath bird-eating tarantula** is the second largest spider in the world. It mosty eats insects, but can grow big enough to eat birds, bats, lizards, and mice.

This giant's legs are longer than this book!

This beautiful, rare spider is called the **gooty sapphire tarantula**. It's also known as the "peacock tarantula" because of its colours. It can only be found in one forest in India.

Gooty sapphire tarantulas are more aggressive than most other tarantulas.

Eight legs (like all spiders)

Octopus alert

With eight arms, these **unusual** underwater animals are easy to recognize. But they're hard to spot because they're good at hiding.

Caribbean reef octopus

Staying hidden

Some octopuses are very good at **hiding** by changing colour and shape to blend in with the sea floor. Others lurk in holes, crevices, and caves.

The blue-ringed octopus is tiny, but it's one of the deadliest animals on earth.

Blue-ringed octopus

Mimic octopus

Common octopus

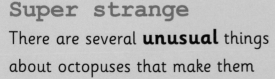

Octopuses don't have any bones, so they can

Super strange

There are several **unusual** things about octopuses that make them very special animals. What are they?

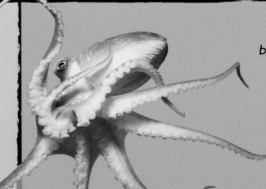

They have no bones, eight arms, blue blood, and three hearts.

Clever creatures

Octopuses are very **intelligent**. Scientists have discovered that they can solve puzzles and escape from mazes.

Giant Pacific octopus

The giant Pacific octopus is bigger than most cars!

squeeze their bodies into even the tiniest of holes.

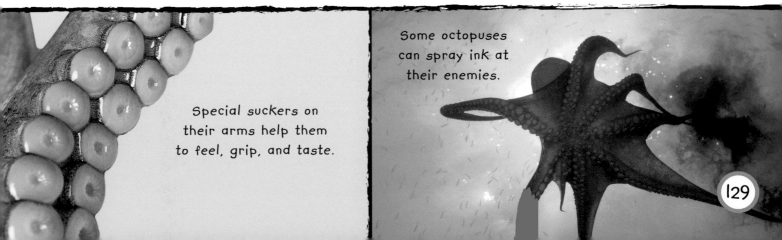

Special suckers on their arms help them to feel, grip, and taste.

Some octopuses can spray ink at their enemies.

Feeling crabby

These shelled creatures look like ocean insects, but crabs are **crustaceans** like lobsters and shrimp. Most crabs can live on land and in water.

Hard shell protects a soft inside.

Hermit crabs

These tiny crabs don't have their own shells for protection, so they search the sea for **empty shells** to move into. It's a little like a crab's version of moving house!

Hermit crabs mostly live in empty sea snail shells or clams, but they've been found using other objects such as plastic lids.

Plastic lid

Sea snail shell

Claw

Fiddler crab

Male fiddler crabs are easy to spot because **one of their claws** is much bigger than the other!

Big claw →

Decorator crab

Decorator crabs have a sneaky skill. They **cover their bodies** in seaweed and sea sponges to hide from enemies.

Seaweed

Most crabs walk sideways instead of forwards.

Japanese spider crab

These monsters are the **giants** of the crab world. They can be found in chilly waters in Japan, and are absolutely huge!

My legs can be longer than a person is tall.

Portuguese man-of-war

Sometimes called the "floating terror", the Portuguese man-of-war is a floating **stinging machine**. Watch out for its tentacles!

One or many?

It may look like a jellyfish, but this strange-looking creature isn't one animal at all — it's a **colony of animals** that live and work together.

Stinging tentacles

The man-of-war's tentacles are **venomous**, and paralyze fish that get tangled up in them. The tentacles are usually about 9m (30ft) long, but they can grow to be five times longer.

Sail

Tentacles

A clever trick

Hardly anything goes near a man-of-war because it is so deadly. But tiny **blue sea slugs** eat man-of-war tentacles and use the venom to protect themselves.

Full of gas

The man-of-war's **sail** is a gas-filled pouch. In bad weather a man-of-war can empty the pouch and quickly disappear underwater.

A man-of-war can't change direction. It justs floats wherever the waves take it.

They're called man-of-wars because their sail looks like the sails on an old type of ship.

Animal antics

Wild animals don't need to go to school, so what do they **get up to**? Well, they spend most of their time looking for food, communicating with each other, moving from place to place, and avoiding enemies. Find out how!

Sticking together

While many wild animals live alone, others gather in big groups called **herds**. They do this for lots of reasons, but the main one is safety.

Most animals that live in herds travel

Reindeer travel together in their thousands across North America, Asia, Europe, and Greenland.

Zebras stay together for safety. It's much easier to keep a look out for lions and hyenas as a group.

and eat together.

Gazelles roam the plains of Africa in search of food. They can gather in groups of a few hundred.

An **elephant** herd is led by the oldest female, and the herd looks after the young together.

Unlikely friends

Although lots of animals stick to their own kind, sometimes two **very different** animals will help each other out.

Sea anemone tentacles can cause a painful sting. But **clownfish** aren't affected by it. The clownfish keep the anemone clean, and the anemone keeps the clownfish safe.

Sea anemone

Clownfish

When **aphids** suck sap from plants, they produce something called honey dew. **Ants** love honey dew so much that they protect the aphids.

Remoras are fish with suckers on their heads that stick to **sharks**. The sharks get cleaned, and the remora gets to eat any food left by the sharks.

Cattle egrets are birds that perch on big animals such as **buffalo** and hippos. The egrets eat insects that bother or disturb the big animals.

Ostriches have great eyesight, and **zebras** have a strong sense of smell. Together, they make an effective team looking out for danger.

A penguin story

Life isn't always easy for **emperor penguins**. Adult penguins have to struggle through bitterly cold winters to raise their chicks.

During the autumn mating season, a female penguin lays a single egg.

The male takes the egg and looks after it. He keeps it **warm** by holding it between his feet and a special fold of skin.

The female leaves for around two months in winter to **find food**. She has to walk for miles to reach the sea, where she eats as many fish as she can.

It gets so cold that the male penguins all **huddle** together to keep warm. They take it in turns to be in the middle of the group where it is warmest.

When the female returns, she calls to her mate and the family is reunited. The female feeds the newly hatched **chick** and the male takes his turn to get food.

Time to **sleep**

Just like people, animals need to **rest**.
And while some creatures only take short
naps, others sleep almost all day long!

Animals sleep more in zoos than

The eucalyptus leaves
koalas eat don't give
them much energy, so
koalas need a lot of rest.
They can sleep for up
to 18 hours a day!

Bats sleep upside down.
When they wake up they drop
into the air and fly away.

Snakes can't close their
eyes, so it's hard to know
when a snake is asleep!

Dolphins never go into
deep sleep because they
need to be awake to breathe.
So when a dolphin sleeps,
half of its brain stays awake.

ZZZZZZ

Whale rested

Sperm whales take short naps through the day. They sleep **upright** near the water's surface so they can breathe.

I sleep for about 10 hours a night.

We hardly ever stop to sleep!

Ants are hard workers. They only rest or take short naps through the day.

in the wild.

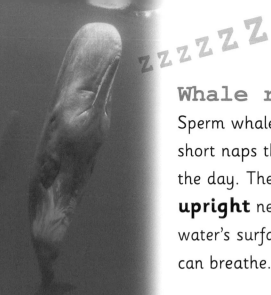

Armadillos are usually active at night. During the day they curl up and sleep for up to 16 hours.

Although **sloths** can seem like real sleepyheads, in the wild they sleep for about 10 hours – not much more than people.

Pigs are social animals. When they sleep, they like to huddle together.

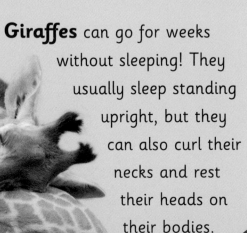

Giraffes can go for weeks without sleeping! They usually sleep standing upright, but they can also curl their necks and rest their heads on their bodies.

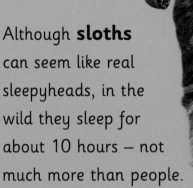

Feeding time
Before hibernation, the animal **eats lots** of food so it has enough energy to last for months.

Time to sleep
The animal goes to sleep in a **burrow**, **nest**, or **cave**. Its body gets very cold and its heart only beats a few times a minute.

Follow me as I get ready for my big, long sleep.

A winter's sleep

Some animals, such as hedgehogs, mice, and chipmunks, sleep all winter. This is because the weather gets cold, and it's hard to find food. This is called **hibernation**.

Months later

The animal wakes up in the **spring**, when it's much warmer and there's more food.

Spring has sprung!

Some birds fly to warmer places instead of hibernating.

A summer's sleep

Some desert animals, such as desert frogs, insects, and snails, sleep most of summer — when it gets too hot for them.

Many bears sleep for most of the winter, but they can wake up quickly, so it's not a true hibernation.

What's for dinner?

All living things need to **eat** food to get the energy they need. But different animals need to eat different things.

Types of diet

Many animals only eat **plants**, but others only eat **other animals**. Some animals (including people) eat both.

> We're fussy eaters. I only eat bamboo, and koalas only eat eucalyptus leaves.

Koala

> I eat meat, vegetables, and fruit. Some of my friends don't eat meat.

Panda

Meat eaters

Animals that eat other animals are **carnivores**. Many have sharp claws or teeth to help them hunt.

I eat teeny-tiny insects.

Ladybird

Alligator

Owl

Tiger

Shark

Plant eaters

Herbivores are animals that only eat plants. They usually have strong jaws for chewing or cracking.

Macaw

Caterpillar

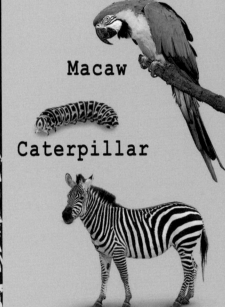

Zebra

Elephant

Cow

Both!

The animals that eat both meat and plants are called **omnivores**. Most people are omnivores.

Squirrel

Ostrich

Pig

Ants

Hedgehog

I like to eat insects and berries.

Black bear

Food chain

All animals need **energy**, which they get from the food they eat. Most of this energy gets passed from animal to animal in a process called a food chain.

Food webs

Animals eat lots of different types of food, so there are lots of different food chains. When food chains **link together** they can create complex food webs.

Hawk

5

Finally, a hawk might eat the snake. Very few animals hunt hawks, so it is at the end (top) of the food chain.

4

Snakes and other predators eat frogs and smaller animals.

Snake

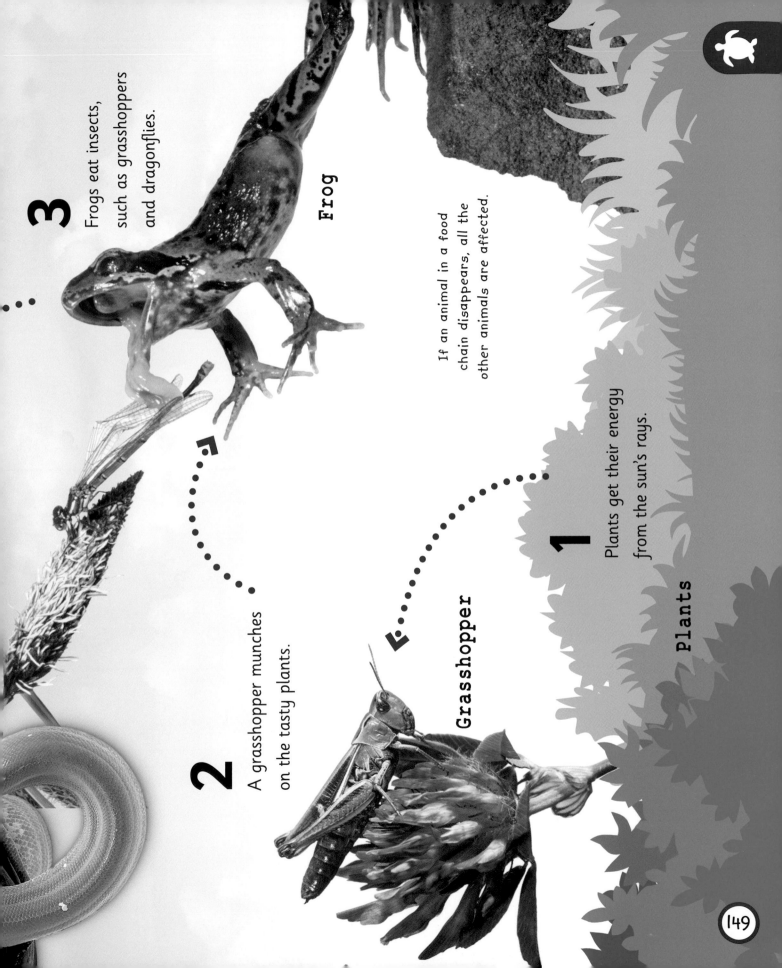

3

Frogs eat insects, such as grasshoppers and dragonflies.

Frog

If an animal in a food chain disappears, all the other animals are affected.

2

A grasshopper munches on the tasty plants.

Grasshopper

1

Plants get their energy from the sun's rays.

Plants

149

Taking a trip

Many animals make **long journeys** to escape bad weather, find food, and breed. These journeys are called **migrations**.

Arctic tern

Start: The Arctic
Finish: Antarctica

These birds fly from the Arctic to Antarctica – all the way on the **other side of the world** – to mate. Then they fly back again!

Arctic terns travel further than any other animal.

Red crab

Start: The forest
End: The ocean

Each year, millions of red crabs on **Christmas Island**, near Australia, travel from the forest to the ocean to lay their eggs.

Roads on the island are closed to let the crabs cross.

Monarch butterfly

Start: Canada
End: Mexico

Some monarch butterflies fly south along the coast of North America to escape the **cold**. Once they arrive at the end of their journey they lay their eggs and their babies fly back again.

Humpback whale

Start: Arctic waters
End: Tropical waters

Humpback whales travel thousands of miles a year. In the summer they go to **cold** waters where there's lots of food. Then in the winter, they swim to **warm** waters to have their babies.

Twit-twoo! I'm hiding. What other animals are hiding on these pages?

Bush cricket that looks like a brown leaf.

Hide and seek

Some animals are masters at blending in with their surroundings. This is called **camouflage** and it's a useful skill for hunting or for hiding.

The stripy pattern on a **tiger** doesn't just look impressive. It helps the tiger stay hidden amongst tall grass, and sneak up on unsuspecting prey.

Stick insects can hide amongst sticks. They look so much like twigs that when they stand still none of their enemies can tell the difference!

Butterfly that looks like a green leaf.

Snake hiding in the leaves.

Animals such as **stoats** and **polar bears** that live in places with cold, snowy winters often have white fur to blend in with the snow.

The **leaf-tailed gecko** has a body that looks like a rotten leaf. It clings to branches, and blends in with the bark and leaves to avoid being eaten.

Underwater camouflage

The ocean is a mysterious place. Living there can be tough, so these animals have adapted to **hide** in **plain sight**.

This strange fish looks like seaweed!

Stonefish can look just like coral or the seabed. It uses its camouflage to hunt – it lies still and waits to attack.

The **mimic octopus** has a unique form of camouflage. It can change shape to look like other animals!

I'm a scorpionfish. I'm great at hiding in coral.

The **cuttlefish** can change its colour to blend in with its background. It can pretend to be coral, rocks, or sand!

The **peacock flounder** can change its colour and its pattern to match the colour of the seabed.

On defence

What do animals do when a predator is nearby? Well these animals have impressive ways of **protecting** themselves.

Scaly plates protect **armadillos** like armour. Some armadillos can roll themselves up into a tight ball.

Pufferfish inflate their bodies with water. This makes them too big and spiky for predators to swallow them.

Prairie dogs stand guard to watch out for enemies. If they see any, they make noise to warn others of the danger.

| Strong armour | Change size | Alarm system |

Don't tell anyone, but I'm alive!

Porcupines have lots of needle-like quills on their backs. Animals that attack are met with nasty spikes.

If they feel threatened, **skunks** can spray their attackers with a liquid that creates a very strong, bad smell.

The **opossum** tricks predators into thinking they're dead. When the attacker leaves, they go back to normal!

Spiky surprise

Bad smell

Playing dead

Venom or poison?

Sharp teeth and claws aren't the only ways animals can be **deadly**. They can also be poisonous or carry a nasty venom. What's the difference?

Venom

Animals that **inject** a deadly substance by biting, stinging, or scratching are venomous. They do this to catch food or defend themselves from attackers.

I'm a scorpion. My tail has a sting with a strong venom.

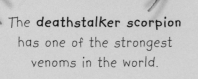

The **deathstalker scorpion** has one of the strongest venoms in the world.

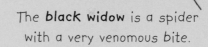

The **black widow** is a spider with a very venomous bite.

The **king cobra** is the world's largest venomous snake. It injects venom through its sharp fangs.

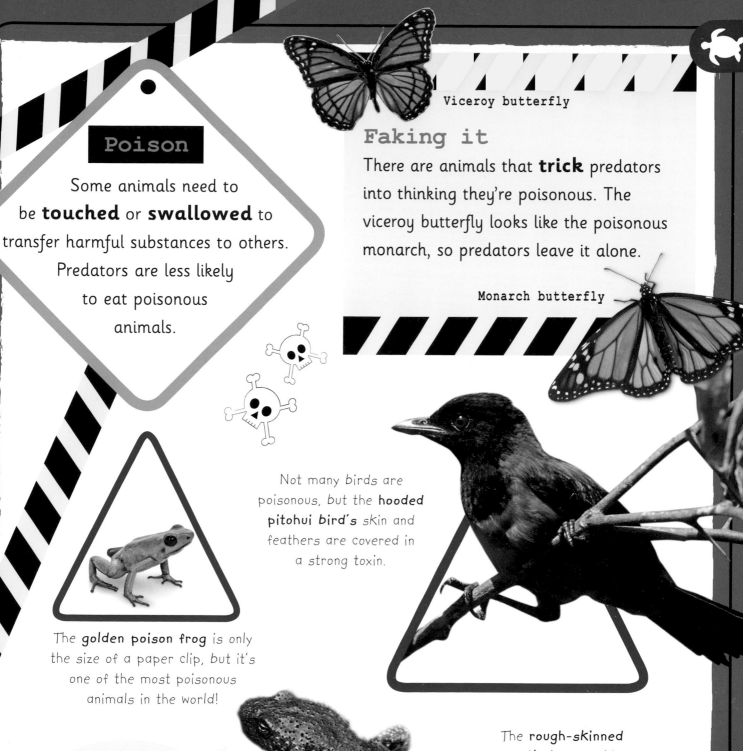

Poison

Some animals need to be **touched** or **swallowed** to transfer harmful substances to others. Predators are less likely to eat poisonous animals.

Viceroy butterfly

Faking it

There are animals that **trick** predators into thinking they're poisonous. The viceroy butterfly looks like the poisonous monarch, so predators leave it alone.

Monarch butterfly

Not many birds are poisonous, but the **hooded pitohui bird's** skin and feathers are covered in a strong toxin.

The **golden poison frog** is only the size of a paper clip, but it's one of the most poisonous animals in the world!

Animals don't eat me because they'll get sick.

The **rough-skinned newt's** bumpy skin produces toxins.

Let's move!

As well as **running**, **swimming**, and **flying**, animals can get around in lots of other interesting ways.

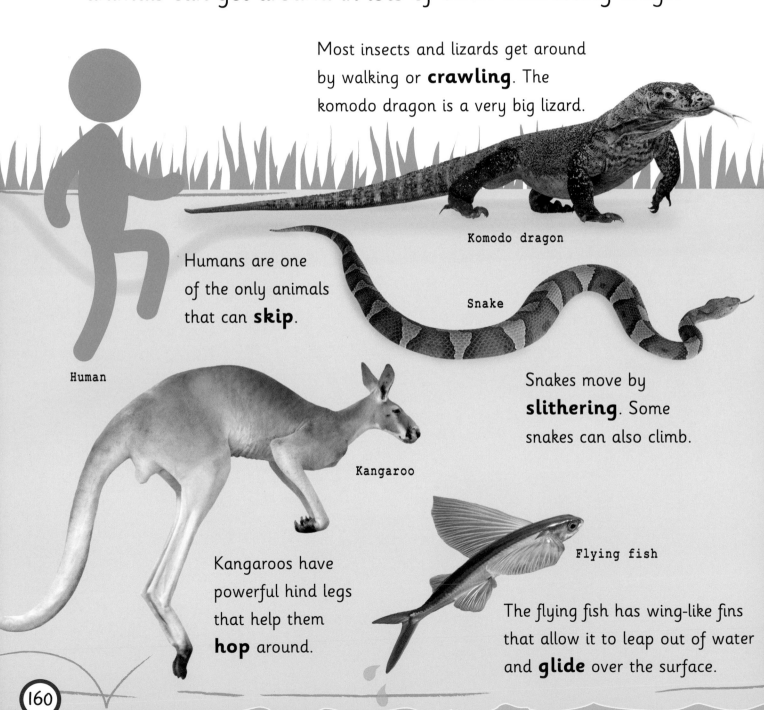

Most insects and lizards get around by walking or **crawling**. The komodo dragon is a very big lizard.

Komodo dragon

Humans are one of the only animals that can **skip**.

Snake

Human

Snakes move by **slithering**. Some snakes can also climb.

Kangaroo

Flying fish

Kangaroos have powerful hind legs that help them **hop** around.

The flying fish has wing-like fins that allow it to leap out of water and **glide** over the surface.

Gibbon

Fleas are great **jumpers**. They can jump up to 100 times their height!

Flea

Many monkeys and apes use their long arms to **swing** from branch to branch.

Alpine ibex

Penguins have short legs and big feet so they **waddle** around on land. They can **slide**, too!

One type of lemur can do a funny **dance**!

The alpine ibex is an expert **climber**. It can climb steep cliffs thanks to its special hooves.

Penguin

Lemur

Geckos have special hairs on their feet for **climbing**.

Jerboa

The jerboa uses its hind legs to **hop**, and lands on its front paws.

Mudskipper

The mudskipper fish can leave water and **drag** itself on land using its fins as arms.

Gecko

Using tools

Some animals have **learned** how to use tools to get food, protect themselves, or just make their lives a little bit easier.

Sea otters use rocks to smash open the hard shells of crabs, clams, oysters, and sea urchins before they eat them.

I wave my anemones like a cheerleader waves pom-poms!

Anemones sting, so **pom-pom crabs** sometimes pick up an anemone in each claw and use them as weapons.

Finches on the Galapagos islands poke cactus spines into trees and cacti to fish insects out of their hiding places.

Veined octopuses make a shelter from empty coconuts and seashells so they can hide from any attackers.

I need a giant stick to scratch that itch on my back.

Elephants use branches to scratch their backs. They also use leaves to fan away flies that buzz around them.

Gorillas check if a river or lake is safe to cross by poking a long stick in the water to test how deep it is.

Sounds of the **wild**

One way that animals communicate is with sound, and they can be very **noisy**. Meet some of the loudest and find out what all the racket is about!

roar!

howl!

A **lion's** roar is one of nature's most impressive sounds. Lions roar to warn off rival males. The sound is so loud, it can be heard from 8 km (5 miles) away.

The shrieks of a **howler monkey** are as loud as a passing motorbike. Just imagine what it sounds like when they get together with their friends!

Cricket

chirp chirp

Not only am I the biggest animal in the world. I'm one of the loudest too!

Blue whales sing a whistling tune to communicate with other whales. Their calls can be almost as loud as a rocket taking off!

chirp chirp

Cicadas are insects that make a chirping, buzzing sound. A single cicada isn't very loud, but when they gather in their millions the noise is deafening!

trumpet! trumpet!

Elephants make trumpeting sounds when they're excited, warning others of danger, or being aggressive. They can be heard 9 km (6 miles) away.

On Madagascar

Madagascar is an island off the coast of Africa. It is famous for some of the most **special** wildlife found anywhere in the world.

Crested coua

Tomato frog

Madagascan dwarf chameleon

White-footed sportive Lemur

Chameleons

Around **half** the world's chameleons live on Madagascar, including a chameleon so small that it can fit on a fingernail!

Madagascar

Satanic leaf-
tailed gecko

One home

Some animals only live in one place.
We call these animals **"endemic"**.
Three out of four animals on Madagascar
aren't found anywhere else on Earth.

Indri

Ring-tailed lemur

Lots of lemurs

Lemurs are a group of **primates** that
only live on Madagascar. No one knows
for sure how they got to the island, but
they've been there for thousands of years.

Giraffe
weevil

Darwin's big trip

A long time ago, a young man called Charles Darwin set off on a sailing trip. Along the way he made one of the most important animal **discoveries** of all time.

Darwin's trip started in England. He travelled on the ship, the **HMS Beagle**. He spent more than five years travelling to different places.

When the Beagle landed, Darwin collected fossils and **studied nature**. He observed many different types of plants and animals.

← Finches

Darwin's most important discovery came when he visited the **Galapagos Islands**, near South America. He noticed that animals such as finches and mockingbirds were slightly **different** on each island.

Darwin realized that the finches had **changed** over millions of years and **adapted** to their different island habitats.

No, no, no! Darwin is all wrong!

Darwin wrote about his discoveries, but for years many people didn't believe him. Today, Darwin's discoveries are considered to be very important.

A helping hand

Animals do a lot of things to help us such as making food for us to eat and materials for clothes. Even their poo can be **useful**!

Silkworm in a cocoon.

Silkworms make **silk**, which is a fabric we use to make clothes and kites.

Honeybees go from flower to flower, collecting a liquid called nectar. They turn this liquid into **honey**. Bees also carry pollen, which is good for plant growth.

Honey

Birds lay **eggs**. Chicken eggs are the most popular, but people also eat duck eggs, huge ostrich eggs, and tiny quail eggs.

Chickens lay an egg about once a day.

In hot weather, sheep, goats, and alpacas' fleeces are sheared off and turned into **wool**. We make clothes from the wool.

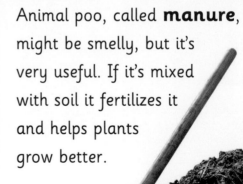

Many animals make **milk**. Cows milk is popular, but many people drink goat, buffalo, camel, and horse milk as well.

Milk can also be used to make cheese.

Animal poo, called **manure**, might be smelly, but it's very useful. If it's mixed with soil it fertilizes it and helps plants grow better.

171

Animals and us

There are some **jobs** that animals are good at helping us with. Luckily, our animal friends are around when we need them.

Some animals, such as this police horse, have jobs. Just like people!

Guide dogs are trained to help people who can't see very well. They can help people to cross the street, find where they're going, and use buses and trains.

Carrier pigeons can find their way home – even if they're far away. People attach notes to their legs and let them fly off to deliver the messages.

I'm off to deliver a message!

Camels are great at carrying heavy loads through the desert.

Before we had cars, people relied on animal power. **Horses**, **camels**, and **donkeys** are faster and stronger than us, and can pull or carry heavy things.

A **sheep dog** is trained to control sheep and tell them where to go. The dog runs around the sheep, but never harms them. This is called "herding".

animals

These next pages tell you about **even more cool creatures**. So take a peek to discover everything from the different noises animals make, which animals have spots or stripes, to the places animals live, and much more.

Lots of spots

All kinds of animals, whether they live in the sea, sky, or on land, can have **spots**. Some animals use their spots to hide, and others use them as a warning.

Magpie moth

Spotty cat

Cheetahs are the fastest land animals on Earth. Their spots help them blend in amongst grass while they are hunting.

Spotty amphibians

Ornate horned frog

Poison dart frogs

The **greater spotted woodpecker** has spots on its wings. You can see them when it flies.

Spotty bird

Spotty fish

Spotted lizards

Spotty reptile

Pufferfish

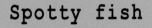

Harlequin sweetlips fish

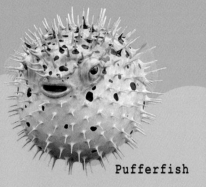

Blue-spotted stingray

Panther grouper

Spotty insect

Ladybirds

Spotty dog

Dalmatian puppies are born white — their spots only appear as they grow. Some Dalmatians have spots inside their mouths!

Lots of stripes

Spots aren't the only pattern that animals can have — many of them are covered from head to toe in **stripes**.

Bumblebee buzzzzzzz

Striped mammals

Zebra

Each **zebra** has a unique set of stripes, so no two zebras look exactly the same. Their stripes can confuse predators when they are being chased.

Chipmunk

Brazilian tapir baby

Tapir babies are born with stripes and spots. This helps to keep them hidden.

Striped amphibians

Caecilian

Fire salamander

Striped invertebrates

Striped millipede

Minstrel bug

Staudinger's longtail moth

Striped fish

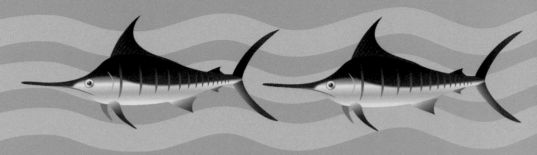

Striped marlins have silver and blue bodies and purple stripes.

Striped reptiles

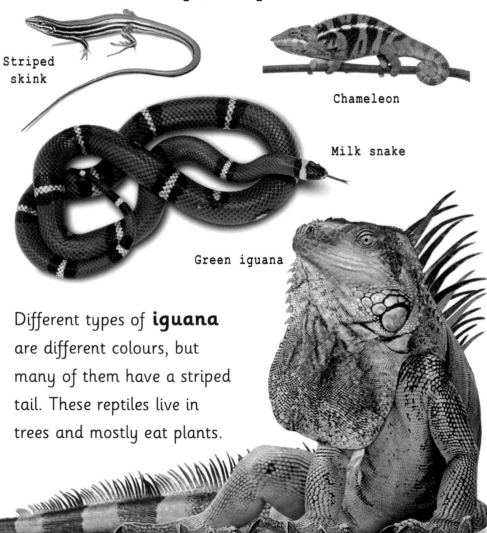

Striped skink

Chameleon

Milk snake

Green iguana

Different types of **iguana** are different colours, but many of them have a striped tail. These reptiles live in trees and mostly eat plants.

Crazy colours

The animal kingdom is bursting with a **rainbow** of colour. Some animals are colourful because they want to be noticed, but others use it as a warning.

Orangutan

Starfish

Panther chameleon

Jewel wasp

Rainbow lorikeet

Giant centipede

Giant atlas moth

Blue-footed booby

Golden pheasant

Crab spider

Macaw

Peacock butterfly

Mandrill

Ring-necked snake

Gecko

Discus fish

I've got a very powerful punch. My bright colours warn enemies away.

Poison dart frog

Thorn bug

Flamingo

Jewel weevil

Mantis shrimp

Blue morpho butterfly

Peacock

Clownfish

Toucan

Going under

These animals are burrowers, which means they **dig** underground. They can dig small holes to hide in or huge tunnels to live in.

Groundhog

Tarantula

Jerboas make small burrows in the desert.

Jerboa

Rabbit

Wombat

Badger

Brilliant builders

Some talented animals can make their own structures. Whether it's a safe nest to raise a family, or a warm winter hideout, these animals are **super builders**.

Paper wasp

We beavers work together to build dams and homes using branches, mud, and rocks.

Beaver

Weaver bird

I'm a male bowerbird. I build a special nest to impress females.

Weaver ants

Bowerbird

I hide inside my web and wait for tasty prey to walk in.

Funnel web spider

Harvest mouse

Ovenbird

Divers

What do these animals have in common?
They spend a lot of their time diving
into the sea, but none of them
can breathe underwater.

Cape gannet

The Cape gannet dives
into water at huge speeds,
then uses its wings to
"swim" underwater.

**Bottlenose
dolphin**

**Marine
iguana**

**South American
fur seal**

I can dive deeper
than almost any other
mammal in the world.

**Sperm
whale**

When I dive into water, I can stay there for almost an hour without coming up for air.

Emperor penguin

Brown pelican

Weddell seal

Yellow-lipped sea krait

Leatherback turtle

Polar bear

Pilot whale

Super soarers

It's hard work flapping your wings all day! That's why some birds spread their wings to glide and **soar**, letting warm air currents do the work.

Short-tailed hawk

Albatross

I belong to a group of birds called gulls. We're seabirds, and we're expert gliders.

Kittiwake

Tawny eagle

188

A little lift

Soaring birds rely on **warm air** to stay in the sky, rather than flapping their wings. They spread their wings and the rising warm air lifts them up.

Andean condor

Bridled tern

Stork

Indian vulture

Ravens

Ravens flap their wings less and glide more than most small birds.

Built for **speed**

While the very fastest animals in the world get around by flying, these rapid **runners** can also move around quickly.

Hare

Lion

Horse

I'm the fastest runner on Earth. Only a few birds fly faster than I run.

Cheetah

Wildebeest and pronghorns need to be quick so they can run away from predators.

Wildebeest

Cockroach

Cockroaches and tiger beetles may be small, but they move very quickly.

Pronghorn

Tiger beetle

Ostrich

Climbers

Whether they climb **rocks**, **trees**, or even **walls**, these adventurous animals clearly don't have a fear of heights!

I'm a nubian ibex. I find it easy to balance on steep cliffs.

Cat

Sloth

Snake

Snail

Crabs

Geckos can cling to almost any surface.

Gecko

Squirrel

Orangutans

Mountain animals

Some animals love the **high life**.
These creatures live in mountain forests,
or on rocky or snowy mountain cliffs.

A snow leopard's
fur blends into its
high, rocky home.

Red panda

Snow leopard

Alpine
ibex

Kea

Grey wolf

Lanner falcon

Bearded
vulture

I live in the mountains of South America. My thick hairy coat keeps me warm.

Coyote

Llama

Barbary macaque

Pumas are also known as cougars or mountain lions.

Puma

Yak

Desert dwellers

Deserts are places with very **little water**.
It's hard to survive there, but these creatures
have still made the desert their home.

Roadrunner

Oryx

Golden
jackal

Spiny
mouse

There isn't much food in
the desert. So it's a good
thing I can go for months
without eating.

Web-footed
gecko

Scorpion

196

I can drink a lot of water at once, then survive without drinking for months.

Camel

Beige fashion

Lots of desert animals have light-coloured fur, feathers, or scales. This helps to **reflect the sun** and keep them cool.

Meerkat

Sandgrouse

Tortoise

Many desert animals spend the hottest part of the day keeping cool in the shade.

Diadem snake

Trip to the tropics

They're hot, wet, and exploding with life!

Tropical **rainforests** are home to almost half the life on Earth.

Blue morpho butterfly

Great hornbill

Scarlet macaw

Parakeet

Capuchin monkey

Hoooooooooooooowl!

Howler monkeys

Green tree python

Toucan

Sloth

The very top layer of the trees in the rainforest is called the **emergent** layer.

The **canopy** is high up in the trees, where there are lots of branches.

Red-eyed
tree frog

Jaguar

Anteater

Tapir

Rainforests are
split into four
different layers.

Leafcutter
ants

The **understory**
is covered with
growing trees
and shrubs.

Chimpanzee

The **forest floor**
is home to the animals
that don't climb trees.

Capybaras

199

Wild woodlands

If you go down to the **woods** today, you might just bump into one of these animals. Keep your eyes peeled to see who you might spot in the forest.

Crossbill

Chipmunk

Fox

Echidna

I'm a muntjac deer, which is a very small member of the deer family.

Stag beetle

Deer

I'm a black bear. I climb trees to look for food or a place to sleep.

Woodpecker

Bear

Rabbits

Badger

Squirrel

Owl

Raccoons and foxes like to live in forests, but you can also find us in cities.

Raccoon

Ants

The coral reef

Coral reefs are like the **rainforests** of the sea. They're only a small part of the oceans, but more marine animals live there than anywhere else.

Sea turtle

Sea krait

Sea sponge

I eat the algae that lives on coral, then poo out white sand!

Parrotfish

Open anemone

Clownfish

Closed anemone

Strawberry anemone

Giant clam

Blacktip reef shark

Cuttlefish

Emperor angelfish

Spotted eagle ray

Male seahorses look after their young. The females don't.

Spotted seahorse

I like hiding in rocky dens amongst the coral.

What is coral?

It may look like rock, but coral is made up of lots of tiny living animals called **polyps**. Polyps have a hard skeleton to protect themselves.

Coral

Moray eel

Polar creatures

Although it's too **cold** for most animals, many creatures live in the **polar regions**. Some live near the North Pole and others near the South Pole.

Snowy owl

Lemming

My fur turns from white to brown for summer.

Arctic fox

Near the North Pole (Arctic)

Snow goose

Arctic hare

Polar bear

Walrus

Ribbon seal

I fly all the way from the North Pole to the South Pole and back again!

Arctic tern

Wandering albatross

Antarctic skua

Gentoo penguin

We're tiny but very important! Lots of polar animals rely on us for food.

Krill

Near the South Pole (The Antarctic)

Southern fur seal

Leopard seal

205

On the **farm**

Many farms are used to **grow crops**, such as
wheat, corn, and rice. But you'll also find many
of your favourite animals on and around farms.

Rabbits

My babies are
called kids.

Goat

Pony

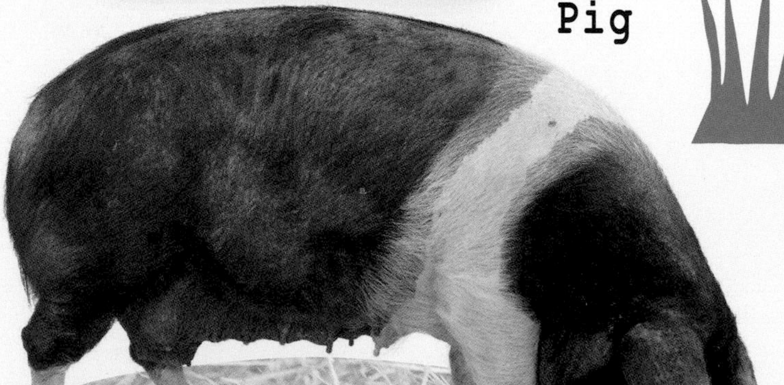

Pig

**Chicken
and chick**

Just like sheep's hair, my hair can be turned into fabrics.

Llama

Sheep and lambs

Turkey

Sheepdog

Cow

Chickens and ducks both lay eggs. Chickens lay about one a day, but we ducks don't lay as many.

Duck

On safari

Stork

The **grasslands** of Africa are full of amazing animals. You never know what wildlife might be peeking out from behind the tall grass.

Leopard

Buffalo

Rhinoceros

I'm a male lion. I have a thick, hairy mane.

African elephant

Lion

Vulture

208

Giraffe

Zebra

Warthog

Springbok

Hippopotamus

We take it in turns to be on guard and watch out for danger.

Meerkats

209

Dazzling dinos

They haven't lived for a long time, but there were once many **different dinosaurs** on Earth. Can you say their names?

> We were around for millions of years, so we didn't all live at the same time.

New discoveries

Everything we know about dinosaurs comes from their **fossilized remains**. Scientists keep studying the fossils so we can learn even more about these creatures.

Sinosauropteryx
(SIGH-no-sore-OP-ter-ix)

Tyrannosaurus
(TIE-ran-oh-SORE-us)

Iguanodon
(ig-GWAH-no-don)

Struthiomimus
(STROO-thee-oh-MIME-us)

Sauropelta
(SORE-oh-PELT-ah)

Giraffatitan
(ji-RAF-a-TIE-tan)

Heterodontosaurus
(HET-er-oh-DON-toe-SORE-us)

Argentinosaurus
(ARE-jen-teen-oh-SORE-us)

Spinosaurus
(SPINE-oh-SORE-us)

Parasaurolophus
(PA-ra-SORE-oh-LOAF-us)

Perfect pets

Although some animals are wild, others make friendly **companions** that live in our homes. Here are some popular pets.

Cats

Keeping pets

All pets need to be well **looked after** and cared for. It's important for pet owners to understand what their pets need.

We need a lot of exercise and love our daily walks.

Dogs

Lizard

Hamster

Goat

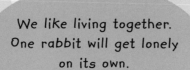
We like living together. One rabbit will get lonely on its own.

Guinea pig

Rabbits

Fish

Bird

Snake

I need a special lamp to keep me hot when it gets cold outside.

Tortoise

Ferret

Animal sounds

Animals can't talk the way people can, but they can **communicate** with each other. One way is by making sounds. How many animals noises do you know?

Bats
SCREECH

Snakes
HISS

Bears
GROWL

Walruses
GROAN

Cats
MIAOW

Howler monkeys
HOWL

Geese
HONK

Other ways
Sound isn't the only way animals communicate. Some animals do it by **changing colour**, **dancing**, or **playing**.

Chameleons change colour to communicate with each other.

Magpies **CHATTER**

Elephants **TRUMPET**

Lions **ROAR**

Dogs **BARK**

What's in a **name?**

Lots of animals like to spend time together. **Groups** of animals can have special names.

BLOAT
of hippos

FLAMBOYANCE
of flamingos

PACK
of wolves

GAGGLE
of geese

CLOUD
of bats

DAZZLE
of zebras

PRIDE
of lions

PARLIAMENT
of owls

TOWER
of giraffes

PRICKLE
of porcupines

CLOWDER
of cats

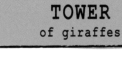

SCHOOL
of fish

MURDER
of crows

AURORA
of polar bears

Animal words

A lot of **important** animal words appear in this book. If you ever get stuck, here's what they mean.

Gecko

Geckos are reptiles.

Aquatic An animal that spends most or all of its life in water. Also a plant that grows in water.

Amphibians A group of cold-blooded animals that can live in water and on land.

Birds A group of warm-blooded animals that hatch from eggs, have feathers, and a beak.

Bone A hard material that makes up the internal skeleton of most vertebrates.

Camouflage Colours or patterns on an animal's body that help it to hide.

Carnivore An animal that only eats meat.

Cold-blooded An animal that can't control its body temperature by internal means.

Colony A group of animals of the same species that live together.

Echolocation A special way that some animals can use reflected sound (echoes) to see.

Endangered An animal at risk of becoming extinct.

Endoskeleton An internal skeleton.

Exoskeleton An external skeleton.

Extinct When there are no more animals in a species left.

Fish A group of mostly cold-blooded aquatic animals that live in water. Many have scales.

Fossil Evidence of past life of a plant or animal that has been preserved in the Earth.

Habitat An animal's natural home environment.

Red panda

Red pandas are endangered. There are not many of them left.

Herbivore An animal that only eats plants.

Hibernation When an animal goes into a deep sleep over winter, where its body temperature and heart rate fall to a low level.

Invertebrate An animal that doesn't have a backbone.

Mammals A group of warm-blooded animals that have hair and drink their mother's milk as babies.

Migration A seasonal movement where animals travel from one place to another and return.

Nocturnal An animal that is active at night.

Omnivore An animal that eats plants and meat.

Poison A harmful substance that can be deadly if touched or eaten.

Baby orangutan

Predator An animal that hunts other animals for food.

Prey An animal that is hunted for food.

Primates A group of mammals including monkeys, apes, lemurs, and humans.

Reptiles A group of cold-blooded animals that hatch from eggs and have scales.

Scales Mainly rigid plates seen on animals such as insects, fish, reptiles, birds, and one mammal (pangolin).

Scavenger An animal that eats dead and dying animals. Some animals today also scavenge human rubbish.

Orangutans are primates.

Species A group of similar animals that share the same features and can have babies together.

Venom A harmful substance that can be injected into an animal through a bite or a sting.

Vertebrate An animal that has a backbone.

Warm-blooded An animal that can control its body temperature.

Vulture

Hermit crab

Crabs have exoskeletons.

Vultures are scavengers.

Index

A

alligators 26, 98–99, 147
amphibians 28–29, 32, 108, 112, 176, 178
anteaters 70–71, 199
ants 30, 41, 70, 71, 138, 143, 183, 185, 201
apes 66, 76, 161
aphids 138
aquatic animals 16–17
arachnids 31
armadillos 143, 156
arthropods 30–31
axolotls 112–113

B

babies 20, 23, 27, 76, 80, 83, 101, 178
bats 18, 21, 74–75, 142
bears 20, 53, 64–65, 145, 147, 153, 187, 201, 204, 214
beavers 56–57, 184
bees 18, 30, 41, 116–117, 170
beetles 30, 37, 40, 121, 191
birds 22–23, 32, 36, 42–43, 80–89, 140–141, 159, 213
birds of paradise 88–89
black panthers 73
bones 36–39, 40, 41, 42
bowerbirds 185
breathing 13, 17, 24

burrowing animals 182–183
butterflies 19, 41, 122–123, 151, 153, 159, 181, 198

C

caecilians 29, 178
camels 173, 197
camouflage 64, 107, 115, 118–119, 128, 152–155
carnivores 147
cats 72–73, 192, 212, 214, 217
cattle egrets 139
centipedes 31, 180
chameleons 102–103, 166, 179, 180, 215
cheetahs 72, 176, 190
chickens 19, 171, 206, 207
chimpanzees 66–67, 199
clownfish 17, 138, 181, 202
cold-blooded animals 25, 27, 29
colonies 116–117, 124, 132
colour changes 103, 107, 128
colourful animals 180–181
communication 59, 67, 121, 164–165, 214–215
coral reefs 202–203
cows 147, 171, 207
crabs 17, 31, 37, 130–131, 150, 162, 193

crocodiles 26, 98–99
crustaceans 31, 130

D

Darwin, Charles 168–169
deer 15, 136, 200
defences 156–157
deserts 34, 35, 196–197
dinosaurs 45, 48–49, 51, 210–211
diving 186–187
dogs 12, 15, 53, 62–63, 172, 173, 177, 207, 212, 215
dolphins 17, 58, 142, 186

E

eagles 19, 86–87, 188
echolocation 75
eels 16, 203
eggs 23, 27, 28, 43, 80, 83, 100–101, 108, 116, 123, 125, 140, 150, 151, 171
elephants 21, 38–39, 46, 53, 68–69, 137, 147, 163, 165, 208, 215
emus 22
endangered animals 52–53
energy 13, 146, 148
extinct animals 50, 53

F

farm animals 206–207
feathers 23, 43, 80, 81
finches 163, 169
fins 25, 58
fireflies 120–121
fish 17, 24–25, 32, 90–95, 177, 179, 213, 217
fleas 161
flight 18–19, 21, 41, 42, 74, 87, 188–189
flying fish 160
food 146–149
food chains and webs 148–149
forests 32, 33
fossils 45, 48, 50–51, 210
frogs 28, 29, 32, 39, 108–111, 118, 145, 149, 159, 166, 176, 181, 199

G

gazelles 137
geckos 106–107, 119, 153, 161, 167, 193, 196
gills 17, 24, 25, 113
giraffes 39, 143, 209, 217
goats 35, 206, 212
gorillas 14, 53, 163, 216
grasshoppers 149
grasslands 33, 208–209
group names 216–217

H

habitats 32–35, 194–209
hawks 13, 23, 148, 188
hedgehogs 15, 144, 147
herbivores 147
herds 136–137
hibernation 144–145
hippopotamuses 14, 209, 216
horses 172, 173, 190
humans 20, 36, 41, 66, 160
hummingbirds 18, 19, 23, 82

I, J

ibex 161, 192, 194
iguanas 53, 179, 186
insects 30, 160, 177
intelligence 129, 162–163
invertebrates 40–41, 179
jellyfish 16, 37, 40, 132–133
jerboas 161, 182

K

kangaroos 160
katydids 119
keratin 43, 61, 105
king cobras 158
koalas 142, 146
komodo dragons 96–97, 160
krill 205

L

ladybirds 30, 147, 177
leaf insects 118–119
leafy sea dragons 154
lemurs 161, 167
leopards 72, 194, 208
lionfish 25
lions 33, 73, 78–79, 164, 190, 208, 215, 217
lizards 26, 34, 36, 96–97, 102–103, 106–107, 160
llamas 195, 207
lobsters 31, 40

M

macaws 18, 147, 181, 198
Madagascar 102, 166–167
mammals 20–21, 58, 60, 178
mammoths 46
manure 171
meerkats 183, 197, 209
mice 14, 78–79, 144–145, 185, 196
migrations 122–123, 150–151
monkeys 161, 164, 195, 214
mountains 35, 194–195
movement 12, 160–161, 190–193
mudskippers 161
mythical animals 44–45

N, O

newts 28, 159

nocturnal animals 18, 61

oceans 16–17, 34, 90–93, 128–131, 154–155, 186–187, 202–203

octopuses 17, 34, 128–129, 154, 163

omnivores 147

opossums 157

orangutans 76–77, 180, 193

orcas (killer whales) 58–59

ostriches 83, 139, 147, 171,191

otters 17, 162

ovenbirds 185

owls 19, 80–81, 147, 201, 217

P

pandas 53, 146, 194

pangolins 60–61

parrotfish 202

peacock flounders 155

penguins 17, 53, 84–85, 140–141, 161, 187, 205

pet animals 212–213

pigeons 172

pigs 15, 143, 147, 206

piranhas 94–95

poisonous animals 111, 158, 159, 176

polar bears 20, 53, 64–65, 153, 187, 204, 217

polar regions 35, 204–205

porcupines 157, 217

Portuguese man-of-war 132–133

prairie dogs 156

praying mantises 114–115

prehistoric animals 46–49, 210–211

pufferfish 156, 177

puffins 19, 23

R

raccoons 201

rainforests 32, 198–199

rattlesnakes 104–105

ravens 189

rays 16, 91, 92–93, 177, 203

remoras 138

reptiles 17, 26–27, 32, 48, 100, 177, 179

S

salamanders 29, 113, 177, 178

scales 24, 25, 60, 61, 156

scorpionfish 155

scorpions 31, 158, 196

sea anemones 37, 138, 162, 202

seahorses 24, 203

seals 17, 59, 186, 187, 204, 205

senses 13

sharks 16, 25, 47, 90–91, 147, 203

silkworms 170

skeletons 21, 36–39, 41

skin shedding 27

skunks 157

sleep 142–145

sloths 143, 192, 198

snails 14, 37, 130, 145, 193

snakes 15, 27, 39, 104–105, 142, 148–149, 153, 158, 160, 179, 181, 187, 193, 197, 198, 202, 213, 214

sounds 164–165, 214–215

species 12

speed 190–191

spiders 15, 31, 41, 126–127, 158, 180, 185

spots and stripes 176–179

squids 16, 45, 121

squirrels 33, 147, 193, 201

stick insects 41, 152

stoats 153

stonefish 154

T

tadpoles 28, 109

tapirs 15, 178, 199

tarantulas 31, 126–127, 182

termites 124–125

terns 150, 189, 205

terrestrial (land) animals 14–15

tigers 21, 47, 53, 73, 147, 152

toads 29, 109

tongues 60, 71, 103, 104
tool use 162–163
tortoises 27, 39, 197, 213
turtles 17, 47, 50, 52, 100–101,
    187, 202

V, W

venom 25, 105, 126, 132, 158
vultures 23, 189, 195, 208
walruses 35, 204, 214
warm-blooded animals 20
wasps 18, 41, 180, 184
weaver birds 184
wetlands 32
whales 52, 143, 151, 165,
    186, 187
what animals are 12–13
wings 18
woodlands 200–201
woodpeckers 23, 177, 201
wool 171
working animals 172–173
worms 37, 40, 120, 183

Z

zebras 136–137, 139, 147,
    178, 209, 217

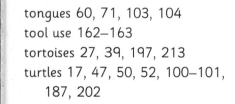

Acknowledgements

The publisher would like to thank the following for their kind permission to reproduce their photographs:

Key: a= above; b=below/bottom; c=centre; f=far; l=left; r=right, t=top.

1 Dorling Kindersley: Jerry Young (cla, crb). **Dreamstime. com:** Jan Martin Will / Freezingpictures (bc). **2 Fotolia:** Star Jumper (r). **3 123RF.com:** smileus (br). **Dorling Kindersley:** Natural History Museum, London (cra). **Photolibrary:** Digital Vision / Martin Harvey (cb). **4 Dorling Kindersley. 5 123RF. com:** Bonzami Emmanuelle / cynoclub (bc). **6 Alamy Stock Photo:** Martin Harvey (crb). **7 123RF.com:** Teri Virbickis (bc). **8 Dorling Kindersley:** Natural History Museum, London (cr). **9 Dorling Kindersley. Fotolia:** uwimages (bc). **10-11 Fotolia:** Dmytro Poliakh / sellingpix (b). **10 123RF.com:** alexiakhruscheva (cla); Eric Isselee (cra/Eurasian red squirrel); Aaron Amat (clb); NejroN (cr); Francisco de Casa Gonzalez (fcrb); Eric Isselee (br). **Dorling Kindersley:** Blackpool Zoo (crb); Jerry Young (fcra); Jerry Young (cra). **11 123RF.com:** Svetlana Foote (c); Eric Isselee / isselee (cla). **Fotolia:** Malbert (b). **12 Dorling Kindersley:** Twan Leenders (bc); Jerry Young (br). **13 Dorling Kindersley:** Stephen Hayward (cl); Natural History Museum, London (clb). **Dreamstime.com:** Eric Isselee (bc). **15 123RF.com:** Volodymyr Krasyuk (cra); Teri Virbickis (br). **16 Alamy Stock Photo:** Martin Strmiska (bl). **Dorling Kindersley:** Jerry Young (cra). **17 123RF. com:** Song Qiuju (clb). **Dorling Kindersley:** Natural History Museum, London (bc/urchin); Linda Pitkin (bc); Jerry Young (c). **Fotolia:** uwimages (cra). **18-19 Fotolia:** Dmytro Poliakh / sellingpix (sky). **19 Dorling Kindersley:** Andrew Beckett (Illustration Ltd.) (ca); Andrew Beckett (Illustration Ltd.) (bl). **21 Dorling Kindersley:** Senckenberg Nature Museum, Frankfurt (cl). **22 Dorling Kindersley:** E. J. Peiker (br). **22-23 Fotolia:** Dmytro Poliakh / sellingpix (grass). **23 123RF.com:** digitaldictator (crb). **Dorling Kindersley:** Alan Murphy (cl); Judd Patterson (ca). **24-25 Fotolia:** rolffimages. **24 123RF.com:** Richard Whitcombe / whitcomberd (cl). **25 123RF.com:** Corey A. Ford (bc). **Dorling Kindersley:** Terry Goss (cr). **26-27 Fotolia:** Malbert (Water). **26 Dorling Kindersley:** Igor Siwanowicz (crb); Jerry Young (cl). **naturepl.com:** John Cancalosi (bc); Bence Mate (cr). **27 123RF. com:** smileus (c). **naturepl.com:** MYN / JP Lawrence (crb). **29 123RF.com:** Pedro Campos (cla). **Dreamstime.com:** Kamnuan Suthongsa (cb). **30 123RF.com:** Aliaksei Hintau / viselchak (tr). **31 123RF.com:** marigranula (cla); Sergio Martínez (crb). **Dorling Kindersley:** Jerry Young (cra). **32 123RF.com:** Eduardo Rivero / edurivero (c). **34 iStockphoto.com:** johnandersonphoto (cr). **35 iStockphoto.com:** goinyk (cr). **36 Science Photo Library:** Arie Van 'T Riet (cra); Science Picture Co (cl). **37 Alamy Stock Photo:** Travis Rowan (crb); Feng Yu (tl). **39 123RF.com:** blueringmedia (ca). **Dorling Kindersley. 40 123RF.com:** Pavlo Vakhrushev / vapi (cr). **Dorling Kindersley:** Jerry Young (bc). **41 Dorling Kindersley:** Jerry Young (cr). **Fotolia:** Eric Isselee (ca). **43 Dorling Kindersley:** Natural History Museum (ca); Natural History Museum, London (clb); E. J. Peiker (cra/Great Blue Heron). **44 Alamy Stock Photo:** Bilwissedition Ltd. & Co. KG (bl); Wildlife GmbH (cl). **iStockphoto.com:** Keith Bishop (tl). **45 Alamy Stock Photo:** North Wind Picture Archives (cla). **iStockphoto.com:** Vasja Koman (br). **46 123RF.com:** Sommai Larkji / sommai (br); sergeyp (br); Katya Ulitina (cra). **Dorling Kindersley:** Royal British Columbia Museum, Victoria, Canada (cl). **47 123RF.com:** artman1 (br); Michael Rosskothen (tc); Mark Turner (c); ramoncarretero (cr). **Dorling Kindersley:** Natural History Museum, London (cb). **naturepl.com:** Jurgen Freund (tr).

48 Dorling Kindersley: Royal Tyrrell Museum of Palaeontology, Alberta, Canada (br). **48-49 123RF.com:** Andrey Armyagov (cb). **50 Dorling Kindersley:** Royal Pavilion & Museums, Brighton & Hove (bc); Senckenberg Gesellshaft Fuer Naturforschugn Museum (crb). **51 Dorling Kindersley:** American Museum of Natural History (c); Natural History Museum (crb). **52 123RF.com:** Andrey Armyagov (crb); Jakub Gojda (Water); Antonio Balaguer Soler (cr). **naturepl.com:** Doug Perrine (bc). **53 123RF.com:** Steven Cooper (cla); Francisco de Casa Gonzalez (tl); Sarah Cheriton-Jones (cra); Berangere Duforets (fcl); donyanedomam (cl); Steven Francis (cr); Volodymyr Goinyk (fcr); Sergei Uriadnikov (br); Joerg Hackemann (bc). **54 Fotolia:** Eric Isselee (cra). **56 123RF.com:** Micha Klootwijk (bc). **57 123RF.com:** Camilo Maranchón garcía (cr); Evgenii Zadiraka (bc). **58 123RF.com:** Mike Price / mhprice (cla). **58-59 123RF.com:** Simone Gatterwe. **60 Alamy Stock Photo:** Reuters (cl). **60-61 Alamy Stock Photo:** Avalon / Photoshot License. **61 Alamy Stock Photo:** Images of Africa Photobank (cla). **naturepl.com:** Michael Pitts (tc). **64 Alamy Stock Photo:** All Canada Photos (c). **Dorling Kindersley:** Jerry Young (cl); Jerry Young (bc). **65 Alamy Stock Photo:** FogStock (c); Wildlife GmbH (clb). **66 Alamy Stock Photo:** Juniors Bildarchiv GmbH (cr). **naturepl.com:** Anup Shah (bl). **66-67 Dreamstime.com:** Glinn (Grass). **67 Alamy Stock Photo:** Eureka (br); Stuart Greenhalgh (c); Martin Harvey (clb). **68 naturepl.com:** Klein & Hubert (tl). **Photolibrary:** White / Digital Zoo (cl). **70 123RF.com:** Valentyna Chukhlyebova (bl). **71 Alamy Stock Photo:** Life on White (cra). **72 Dorling Kindersley:** Wildlife Heritage Foundation, Kent, UK (cb); Jerry Young (cra). **72-73 123RF.com:** Susan Richey-Schmitz (Cheetah). **73 123RF.com:** Anan Kaewkhammul (cra); Anan Kaewkhammul / anankkml (br). **74 123RF.com:** Adi Ciurea (tr); Remus Cucu (tl). **Dorling Kindersley:** Jerry Young (br). **74-75 123RF.com:** xalanx (b). **75 Dreamstime.com:** Ericg1970 (Background). **76-77 123RF.com:** Dejan Stojakovic (b). **76 Fotolia:** Eric Isselee (tr). **77 naturepl. com:** Inaki Relanzon. **80 123RF.com:** jpchret (bl). **82 naturepl. com:** Rolf Nussbaumer (clb); Kim Taylor (cb, cr). **84 123RF.com:** Vladimir Seliverstov (cl). **Getty Images:** Frank Krahmer / Photographer's Choice RF (crb). **85 123RF.com:** Michael Koenen (br); Michael Lane (bl). **Dorling Kindersley:** Peter Anderson (bc/ rock). **Dreamstime.com:** Jan Martin Will / Freezingpictures (bc). **iStockphoto.com:** Keith Szafranski (tr). **86-87 123RF.com:** Ondrej Prosický (c); Radomír Režný (b). **86 123RF.com:** Denise Campbell (bl). **87 naturepl.com:** Angelo Gandolfi (tr). **88 naturepl.com:** Tim Laman (tc); Tim Laman / National Geographic Creative (bc); Tim Laman / National Geographic Creative (cr). **88-89 naturepl.com:** Nick Garbutt (t); Tim Laman (b). **89 123RF.com:** apidach jansawang (r/bark); stillfx (c). **naturepl. com:** Jurgen Freund (cra); Tim Laman / National Geographic Creative (bc); Konrad Wothe (br); Tim Laman / National Geographic Creative (crb); Tim Laman / National Geographic Creative (tr). **90-91 123RF.com:** Didier Brandelet (background). **Alamy Stock Photo:** Brandon Cole Marine Photography. **91 123RF.com:** aquafun (tc); Nicolas Voisin (crb). **Dreamstime. com:** Rhk2222 (cra). **92 123RF.com:** sonet (cb). **naturepl.com:** Alex Mustard (clb); Doc White (tr). **92-93 Dorling Kindersley:** Jerry Young (b/Sand). **naturepl.com:** Pascal Kobeh (b). **93 Dorling Kindersley:** Laszlo S. Ilyes (bl). **94 Alamy Stock Photo:** 1Apix (cl). **95 123RF.com:** Hayati Kayhan; Konstantin Labunskiy (bc). **96-97 123RF.com:** Eric Isselee (c); Eric Isselee (b). **98 naturepl.com:** Doug Wechsler (cla). **98-99 123RF.com:** svetlana foote (b). **99 Dorling Kindersley:** Jerry Young (crb). **100-101 Dorling Kindersley:** David Peart (c).

101 **123RF.com:** Kjersti Jorgensen (br). **102-103 123RF.com:** odmeyer (background). **102 123RF.com:** Eric Isselee (r). **103 123RF.com:** Oxana Brigadirova / Iarus (br). **104-105 Dreamstime.com:** Amwu (c). **105 123RF.com:** Susan Richey-Schmitz (tr). **106-107 Alamy Stock Photo:** Matthijs Kuijpers (b). **106 123RF.com:** Sarayuth Nutteepratoom (cl). **naturepl.com:** Chris Mattison (bl). **107 123RF.com:** Sirichai Raksue (tr); Fedor Selivanov (br). **Alamy Stock Photo:** Chris Mattison (c). **110 123RF.com:** Pedro Campos (bl). **111 123RF. com:** Brandon Alms (cr); weltreisendertj (c); iferol (tc); Dirk Ercken (br); Dirk Ercken (cra); Dirk Ercken (crb); Benoit Daoust (br/ Miniature from). **112 123RF.com:** Vera Kuttelvaserova Stuchelova (b). **iStockphoto.com:** Lumiphil (b). **113 123RF.com:** ekaterinabaikal (cra). **Dorling Kindersley:** Igor Siwanowicz (crb). **114 Alamy Stock Photo:** Nature Production (cl). **naturepl.com:** Nature Production (cl). **115 Alamy Stock Photo:** Nature Picture Library (tr); tbkmedia.de (b). **116 123RF.com:** Jens Brggemann (clb); Yavor Yanakiev (tr). **117 123RF.com:** Subrata Chakraborty (cl); Irina Tischenko (cr). **Alamy Stock Photo:** Scott Camazine (cb). **118 FLPA:** Chien Lee / Minden Pictures (cb). **119 Dorling Kindersley. naturepl.com:** Nick Garbutt (bc). **120 123RF.com:** Oleksii Troianskyi (c). **Alamy Stock Photo:** David Liittschwager / National Geographic Creative (br). **120-121 123RF.com:** Shouhei Fukuda (c). **121 123RF.com:** Oleksii Troianskyi (clb). **naturepl. com:** Nature Production (br). **122 Dorling Kindersley:** Jerry Young (clb). **123 123RF.com:** jhvephotos. **124-125 123RF.com:** Alexander Ludwig. **124 Alamy Stock Photo:** Imagebroker. **125 123RF.com:** Mr. Smith Chetanachan (crb). **Dorling Kindersley:** Blackpool Zoo (tc). **iStockphoto.com:** wckiw (bl). **127 Alamy Stock Photo:** Blickwinkel (bc). **naturepl.com:** MYN / Andrew Snyder (cra). **128 123RF.com:** Toby Gibson (clb). **Dorling Kindersley:** Linda Pitkin (cla). **129 123RF.com:** planctonvideo (br); pr2is (c). **Alamy Stock Photo:** Elisabeth Coelfen Food Photography (bl). **130 123RF.com:** Sirirat Chinkulphithak (cra); Eric Isselee (c). **131 123RF.com:** yarlander (cla). **Getty Images:** Ken Usami (b). **132 Alamy Stock Photo:** Jose B. Ruiz / Nature Picture Library (crb). **132-133 Alamy Stock Photo:** Stephen Frink Collection. **133 Dreamstime.com:** Fred Goldstein (crb). **134 Dorling Kindersley:** Andrew Beckett (Illustration Ltd.) (crb); Natural History Museum, London. **135 iStockphoto.com:** Hajakely (c). **136-137 Alamy Stock Photo:** DAJ Digital Archive Japan; Frans Lanting Studio (b). **136 Alamy Stock Photo:** Frans Lanting Studio (bl). **137 Alamy Stock Photo:** Robertharding (br). **138 123RF.com:** Jozsef Szasz-Fabian (crb). **Dreamstime.com:** Fiona Ayerst (crb). **Fotolia:** uwimages (cla). **139 123RF.com:** Maurizio Giovanni Bersanelli (clb). **Dreamstime.com:** Jamiegodson; Picstudio (clb). **142 123RF.com:** aniramphoto (clb); Alberto Loyo (c); Anastasy Yarmolovich (br). **naturepl.com:** Gerrit Vyn (cr). **143 123RF.com:** Micha Klootwijk (cla); Seubsai Koonsawat (cr). **Alamy Stock Photo:** Wild Wonders of Europe / Lundgren / Nature Picture Library (tl). **naturepl.com:** Nature Production (bc). **144-145 Dorling Kindersley:** Oxford Scientific Films. **144 123RF.com:** Michael Lane (cl). **145 Dreamstime. com:** Miroslav Hlavko (cr). **147 Dorling Kindersley:** Judd Patterson (cl); Jerry Young (cla). **148 Dorling Kindersley:** Judd Patterson (tc). **150 123RF.com:** Alta Oosthuizen (cr). **Alamy Stock Photo:** Auscape International Pty Ltd. (crb); Minden Pictures (br). **151 123RF.com:** Alberto Loyo (tr). **Alamy Stock Photo:** WaterFrame (clb). **152 123RF.com:** josefpittner (l). **Alamy Stock Photo:** blickwinkel (crb). **naturepl.com:** Sandesh Kadur (clb); Konrad Wothe (cra). **153 Dorling Kindersley. iStockphoto.com:** FotoSpeedy. **naturepl.com:** Erlend Haarberg

(clb); Loic Poidevin (crb). **154 123RF.com:** Krzysztof Wiktor (cla); wrangel (clb). **Alamy Stock Photo:** RGB Ventures / SuperStock (crb). **154-155 123RF.com:** Richard Whitcombe (cl). **155 123RF.com:** Joseph Quinn (br); Suwat Sirivutcharungchit (clb). **157 Alamy Stock Photo:** Bruce MacQueen (cr). **158 Dorling Kindersley:** Jerry Young (c). **159 Dorling Kindersley:** Natural History Museum, London (tc); Jan Van Der Voort (b). **naturepl.com:** Daniel Heuclin (c). **160 123RF.com:** Eric Isselee (ca); Anan Kaewkhammul (clb). **naturepl.com:** Brent Stephenson (b). **161 123RF.com:** Matthijs Kuijpers (clb/Jerboa); Ondrej Prosický (fcr); Vladimir Seliverstov (clb); leisuretime70 (bc). **Dorling Kindersley:** Jerry Young (br). **iStockphoto.com:** Hajakely (c). **162 123RF. com:** Jean-Edouard Rozey (clb). **Dreamstime.com:** Piboon Srimak (crb). **163 123RF.com:** Simon Eeman (clb); Colin Moore (tl). **Alamy Stock Photo:** Alex Mustard / Nature Picture Library (tr). **FLPA:** Jurgen & Christine Sohns (crb). **165 Dorling Kindersley:** Natural History Museum, London (clb). **166-167 Dorling Kindersley:** Andrew Beckett (Illustration Ltd.) (b). **166 123RF.com:** Gleb TV (cla); Zdenek Maly (cl); Phattarapon Pernmalai (bl). **Dorling Kindersley:** Jerry Young (cb). **167 123RF.com:** nrey (c); Phattarapon Pernmalai (r). **Dorling Kindersley:** Andrew Beckett (Illustration Ltd.) (br); Natural History Museum, London (bl). **naturepl.com:** Chris Mattison (tr). **168 Dorling Kindersley:** Rebecca Dean (cr); Oxford Museum of Natural History (crb). **Dreamstime.com:** Isselee (tr). **169 Alamy Stock Photo:** Chronicle (t, clb). **Dreamstime.com:** Isselee (cla, ca). **170 123RF.com:** Kostic Dusan (b). **Fotolia:** Norman Pogson (crb). **171 123RF.com:** fedorkondratenko (br); Eric Isselee / isselee (bl). **172 123RF.com:** cylonphoto (clb); Uladzik Kryhin (tl). **Alamy Stock Photo:** Blickwinkel (crb). **173 123RF.com:** Mikkel Bigandt (crb); Phuong Nguyen Duy (clb); Manfred Thürig. **175 Dorling Kindersley:** Jerry Young (tr). **176 123RF.com:** Dirk Ercken (crb). **178 123RF.com:** Marianne Oliva (clb). **Dorling Kindersley:** Gary Ombler (crb). **Fotolia:** Jan Will (cl). **naturepl.com:** Pete Oxford (cra). **179 123RF.com:** 123RFPremium (ca); Eric Isselee (cra); Mr. Suchat Tepruang (cla). **180 123RF.com:** Tim Hester / timhester (c); Keith Levit / keithlevit (cb). **Fotolia:** Photomic (crb). **181 123RF.com:** Bonzami Emmanuelle / cynoclub (cla). **Dorling Kindersley:** Twan Leenders (c); Natural History Museum, London (cb); Jerry Young (clb). **Fotolia:** uwimages (bc). **182 123RF.com:** Oceanfishing (cla). **183 Corbis:** image100 (tr). **Dorling Kindersley:** Blackpool Zoo (br). **184 123RF.com:** Olga Grezova (cra); Anton Starikov (tr); Oleksandr Lytvynenko (cb); Matyas Rehak (cr). **185 123RF.com:** Martin Jose Frade (bc); Saksit Srisuksai (tl); Zarviiolar (c); Rudmer Zwerver (clb); Michael Lane (crb); Beth Partin (bl); Eric Isselee (br); yanukit (cla). **Dreamstime. com:** Michal Candrak (tr); Johncarnemolla (cra). **186 123RF.com:** Hiran Kanthatham (cb); 123RF Premium (cra). **187 123RF.com:** Ishtygashev (clb); Vladimir Seliverstov (ca); leksele (tr); Oxana Lebedeva (fcra). **Dorling Kindersley:** Andrew Beckett (Illustration Ltd.) (cla). **188 Dorling Kindersley:** Hanne and Jens Eriksen (cr); Judd Patterson (cra); The National Birds of Prey Centre (crb). **189 123RF.com:** Ostill (tr). **Dorling Kindersley:** Hanne and Jens Eriksen (cra). **190 123RF.com:** Eric Isselee (cra); Mari art (clb). **191 123RF.com:** Iakov Filimonov (tc); Steve Grodin (cra). **192 123RF.com:** Michaela Dvořáková (cra); Anek Suwannaphoom (crb). **Dreamstime.com:** Vladimir Blinov (c). **193 123RF.com:** Yotrak Butda (tl); Vadym Soloviov (cla); Anan Punyod (cra); Kjersti Jorgensen (crb). **Alamy Stock Photo:** Nature Picture Library (clb). **Dorling Kindersley:** British Wildlife Centre, Surrey, UK (clb). **194 123RF.com:** Eric Issele (cb); Michael Lane (br). **Dorling Kindersley:** Cotswold Wildlife Park

(cla). **195 123RF.com:** Acceptphoto (cl); Michael Lane (c); Renald Bourque (cra); Daniel Prudek (br). **Dreamstime.com:** Nico Smit / EcoSna (tl). **196 123RF.com:** Anan Kaewkhammul (cl); Tom Tietz (cla); Sirylok (cr). **197 123RF.com:** Marigranula (clb); Alta Oosthuizen (c). **198 123RF.com:** Eric Isselee (bl); Kajornyo (tc); Szefei (l/backdrop); Eduardo A Wibowo (cr). **Dorling Kindersley:** Andrew Beckett (Illustration Ltd.) (c). **199 123RF.com:** Anan Kaewkhammul (c). **Dorling Kindersley:** Andrew Beckett (Illustration Ltd.) (cb); Blackpool Zoo, Lancashire, UK (crb). **200 123RF.com:** cla78 (t/backdrop). **Dorling Kindersley:** Jerry Young (cl). **201 123RF.com:** Lynn Bystrom (cla); Eric Isselee (cb). **Dorling Kindersley:** E. J. Peiker (tr). **202 123RF.com:** Isabelle Khn (bl). **Dorling Kindersley:** Linda Pitkin (cb). **202-203 123RF. com:** Mihtiander. **203 Dorling Kindersley:** Linda Pitkin (br). **204 123RF.com:** Vasiliy Vishnevskiy / ornitolog82 (clb). **Dorling Kindersley:** Andrew Beckett (Illustration Ltd.) (ca). **204-205 Dorling Kindersley:** Barnabas Kindersley (t). **205 123RF.com:** Andreanita (ca); Dmytro Pylypenko (cra); Konstantin Kalishko (cl); Dmytro Pylypenko (clb). **Dorling Kindersley:** Andrew Beckett (Illustration Ltd.) (cla). **206 Fotolia:** Eric Isselee (cl). **207 123RF. com:** Bonzami Emmanuelle (cr); Eric Isselee (cla); Hramovnick (t); Petr Vanek (cl). **208 123RF.com:** Duncan Noakes (cra). **Dorling Kindersley:** Jerry Young (cra). **iStockphoto.com:** Nicholas_Dale (tr). **208-209 123RF.com:** Alexandra Giese (t). **209 123RF.com:** Bennymarty (cl); Eric Isselee (ca); Alta Oosthuizen (cb). **Fotolia:** Star Jumper (r). **210 Dorling Kindersley:** Peter Minister (bl). **210-211 Dreamstime.com:** Ollirg (background). **212 123RF. com:** Dmitry Kalinovsky / kadmy (tr). **215 123RF.com:** Eric Isselee (bc); Jukree Boonprasit (ca); Andrey Gudkov (clb); Ostill (fcra). **217 123RF. com:** Brian Kinney (cr); Thomas Samantzis (tc); mhgallery (cra); Tatiana Thomson (c); Magdalena Paluchowska (cla); Igor Korionov (cb); Juan Gil Raga (crb); Vilainecrevette (bl). **219 Fotolia:** Eric Isselee (tc). **220 Dreamstime.com:** Eric Isselee (bc/tiger body). Photolibrary: Digital Vision / Martin Harvey (bc). **221 Dorling Kindersley:** Natural History Museum, London (bl). **224 Dreamstime.com:** Miroslav Hlavko (br)

Cover images: Front: Dorling Kindersley: Natural History Museum, London crb, Jerry Young cla; **Photolibrary:** Digital Vision / Martin Harvey cb

All other images © Dorling Kindersley
For further information see: www.dkimages.com

DK would like to thank:
Martin Copeland, Claire Cordier, Rob Nunn, Surya Sankash Sarangi, Jayati Sood, and Romaine Werblow for picture library assistance, and Marie Lorimer for indexing.

tongues 60, 71, 103, 104

tool use 162–163

tortoises 27, 39, 197, 213

turtles 17, 47, 50, 52, 100–101, 187, 202

V, W

venom 25, 105, 126, 132, 158

vultures 23, 189, 195, 208

walruses 35, 204, 214

warm-blooded animals 20

wasps 18, 41, 180, 184

weaver birds 184

wetlands 32

whales 52, 143, 151, 165, 186, 187

what animals are 12–13

wings 18

woodlands 200–201

woodpeckers 23, 177, 201

wool 171

working animals 172–173

worms 37, 40, 120, 183

Z

zebras 136–137, 139, 147, 178, 209, 217

Acknowledgements

The publisher would like to thank the following for their kind permission to reproduce their photographs:

Key: a= above; b=below/bottom; c=centre; f=far; l=left; r=right; t=top.

1 Dorling Kindersley: Jerry Young (cla, crb). **Dreamstime. com:** Jan Martin Will / Freezingpictures (bc). **2 Fotolia:** Star Jumper (r). **3 123RF.com:** smileus (br). **Dorling Kindersley:** Natural History Museum, London (cra). **Photolibrary:** Digital Vision / Martin Harvey (cb). **4 Dorling Kindersley. 5 123RF. com:** Bonzami Emmanuelle / cynoclub (bc). **6 Alamy Stock Photo:** Martin Harvey (cra). **7 123RF.com:** Teri Virbickis (br). **8 Dorling Kindersley:** Natural History Museum, London (cr). **9 Dorling Kindersley. Fotolia:** uwimages (bc). **10-11 Fotolia:** Dmytro Poliakh / sellingpix (sky). **10 123RF.com:** alexiakhruscheva (cla); Eric Isselee (cra/Eurasian red squirrel); Aaron Amat (clb); NejroN (cr); Francisco de Casa Gonzalez (fcrb); Eric Isselee (br). **Dorling Kindersley:** Blackpool Zoo (crb); Jerry Young (fcra); Jerry Young (cra). **11 123RF.com:** Svetlana Foote (c); Eric Isselee / isselee (cla). **Fotolia:** Malbert (b). **12 Dorling Kindersley:** Twan Leenders (c); Jerry Young (b). **13 Dorling Kindersley:** Stephen Hayward (cl); Natural History Museum, London (clb). **Dreamstime.com:** Eric Isselee (bc). **15 123RF.com:** Volodymyr Krasyuk (cra); Teri Virbickis (br). **16 Alamy Stock Photo:** Martin Strmiska (bl). **Dorling Kindersley:** Eric Isselee (cb). **17 123RF. com:** Song Qiuju (clb). **Dorling Kindersley:** Natural History Museum, London (bc/urchin); Linda Pitkin (bc); Jerry Young (c). **Fotolia:** uwimages (cra). **18-19 Fotolia:** Dmytro Poliakh / sellingpix (sky). **19 Dorling Kindersley:** Andrew Beckett (Illustration Ltd.) (ca); Andrew Beckett (Illustration Ltd.) (bl). **21 Dorling Kindersley:** Senckenberg Nature Museum, Frankfurt (cl). **22 Dorling Kindersley:** E. J. Peiker (br). **22-23 Fotolia:** Dmytro Poliakh / sellingpix (grass). **23 123RF.com:** digitaldictator (crb). **Dorling Kindersley:** Alan Murphy (cl); Judd Patterson (ca). **24-25 Fotolia:** rolffimages. **24 123RF.com:** Richard Whitcombe / whitcomberd (cl). **25 123RF.com:** Corey A. Ford (bc). **Dorling Kindersley:** Terry Goss (br). **26-27 Fotolia:** Malbert (Water). **26 Dorling Kindersley:** Igor Siwanowicz (c); Jerry Young (cl). **naturepl.com:** John Cancalosi (bc); Bence Mate (cr). **27 123RF.com:** smileus (c). **naturepl.com:** MYN / JP Lawrence (crb). **29 123RF.com:** Pedro Campos (cla). **Dreamstime.com:** Kamnuan Suthongsa (c). **30 123RF.com:** Aliaksei Hintau / viselchak (tr). **31 123RF.com:** marigranula (cla); Sergio Martínez (crb). **Dorling Kindersley:** Jerry Young (cra). **32 123RF.com:** Eduardo Rivero / edurivero (c). **34 iStockphoto.com:** johnandersonphoto (cr). **35 iStockphoto.com:** goinyk (cr). **36 Science Photo Library:** Arie Van 'T Riet (cra); Science Picture Co (cl). **37 Alamy Stock Photo:** Travis Rowan (crb); Feng Yu (tl). **39 123RF.com:** blueringmedia (ca). **Dorling Kindersley:** 40 123RF.com: Pavlo Vakhrushev / vapi (cr). **Dorling Kindersley:** Jerry Young (bc). **41 Dorling Kindersley:** Jerry Young (cr). **Fotolia:** Eric Isselee (ca). **43 Dorling Kindersley:** Natural History Museum (ca); Natural History Museum, London (clb); E. J. Peiker (cra/Great Blue Heron). **44 Alamy Stock Photo:** Bilwissedition Ltd. & Co. KG (bl); Wildlife GmbH (cl). **iStockphoto.com:** Keith Bishop (tl). **45 Alamy Stock Photo:** North Wind Picture Archives (cla). **iStockphoto.com:** Vasja Koman (br). **46 123RF.com:** Sommai Larkji / sommai (br); sergeyp (b); Katya Ulitina (cra). **Dorling Kindersley:** Royal British Columbia Museum, Victoria, Canada (cl). **47 123RF.com:** artman1 (br); Michael Rosskothen (tc); Mark Turner (c); ramoncarretero (cr). **Dorling Kindersley:** Natural History Museum, London (cb). **naturepl.com:** Jurgen Freund (tr).

48 Dorling Kindersley: Royal Tyrrell Museum of Palaeontology, Alberta, Canada (br). **48-49 123RF.com:** Andrey Armyagov (cb). **50 Dorling Kindersley:** Royal Pavilion & Museums, Brighton & Hove (bc); Senckenberg Gesellschaft Fuer Naturforschugn Museum (crb). **51 Dorling Kindersley:** American Museum of Natural History (c); Natural History Museum (crb). **52 123RF.com:** Andrey Armyagov (crb); Jakub Gojda (Water); Antonio Balaguer Soler (cr). **naturepl.com:** Doug Perrine (bc). **53 123RF.com:** Steven Cooper (cla); Francisco de Casa Gonzalez (tl); Sarah Cheriton-Jones (cra); Berangere Duforets (fcl); donyanedomam (cl); Steven Francis (cr); Volodymyr Goinyk (fcr); Sergei Uriadnikov (br); Joerg Hackemann (bc). **54 Fotolia:** Eric Isselee (crb). **56 123RF.com:** Micha Klootwijk (bc). **57 123RF.com:** Camilo Maranchón garcía (bl); Evgenii Zadiraka (bc). **58 123RF.com:** Mike Price / mhprice (cla). **58-59 123RF.com:** Simone Gatterwe. **60 Alamy Stock Photo:** Reuters (tl). **60-61 Alamy Stock Photo:** Avalon / Photoshot License. **61 Alamy Stock Photo:** Images of Africa Photobank (cla). **naturepl.com:** Michael Pitts (tc). **64 Alamy Stock Photo:** All Canada Photos (c). **Dorling Kindersley:** Jerry Young (cl); Jerry Young (b). **65 Alamy Stock Photo:** FogStock (cl); Wildlife GmbH (clb). **66 Alamy Stock Photo:** Juniors Bildarchiv GmbH (cr). **naturepl.com:** Anup Shah (bl). **66-67 Dreamstime.com:** Glinn (Grass). **67 Alamy Stock Photo:** Eureka (br); Stuart Greenhalgh (c); Martin Harvey (clb). **68 naturepl.com:** Klein & Hubert (bl). **Photolibrary:** White / Digital Zoo (cl). **70 123RF.com:** Valentyna Chukhlyebova (bl). **71 Alamy Stock Photo:** Life on White (cra). **72 Dorling Kindersley:** Wildlife Heritage Foundation, Kent, UK (cb); Jerry Young (cra). **72-73 123RF.com:** Susan Richey-Schmitz (Cheetah). **73 123RF.com:** Anan Kaewkhammul (cra); Anan Kaewkhammul / anankkml (br). **74 123RF.com:** Adi Ciurea (t); Remus Cucu (tl). **Dorling Kindersley:** Jerry Young (br). **74-75 123RF.com:** xalanx (b). **75 Dreamstime.com:** Ericg1970 (Background). **76-77 123RF.com:** Dejan Stojakovic (b). **76 Fotolia:** Eric Isselee (c). **77 naturepl. com:** Inaki Relanzon (bl). **80 123RF.com:** jpchret (bl). **82 naturepl. com:** Rolf Nussbaumer (clb); Kim Taylor (cb, cr). **84 123RF.com:** Vladimir Seliverstov (cl). **Getty Images:** Frank Krahmer / Photographer's Choice RF (cl). **85 123RF.com:** Michael Koenen (br); Michael Lane (bl). **Dorling Kindersley:** Peter Anderson (bc/rock). **Dreamstime.com:** Jan Martin Will / Freezingpictures (bc). **iStockphoto.com:** Keith Szafranski (tr). **86-87 123RF.com:** Ondrej Prosický (c); Radomír Režný (bl). **87 naturepl.com:** Angelo Gandolfi (tr). **88 naturepl.com:** Tim Laman (tc); Tim Laman / National Geographic Creative (bc); Tim Laman / National Geographic Creative (cr). **88-89 naturepl.com:** Nick Garbutt (t); Tim Laman (b). **89 123RF.com:** apidach jansawang (r/bark); stillfx (c). **naturepl. com:** Jurgen Freund (cra); Tim Laman / National Geographic Creative (bc); Konrad Wothe (br); Tim Laman / National Geographic Creative (bc); Tim Laman / National Geographic Creative (cr). **90-91 123RF.com:** Didier Brandelet (background). **Alamy Stock Photo:** Brandon Cole Marine Photography. **91 123RF.com:** aquafun (tc); Nicolas Voisin (crb). **Dreamstime. com:** Rhk2222 (cra). **92 123RF.com:** sonet (cb). **naturepl.com:** Alex Mustard (cla); Doc White (tr). **92-93 Dorling Kindersley:** Jerry Young (b/Sand). **naturepl.com:** Pascal Kobeh (b). **93 Dorling Kindersley:** Laszlo S. Ilyes (bl). **94 Alamy Stock Photo:** 1Apix (cl). **95 123RF.com:** Hayati Kayhan; Konstantin Labunskiy (bc). **96-97 123RF.com:** Eric Isselee (c); Eric Isselee (b). **98 naturepl.com:** Doug Wechsler. **98-99 123RF.com:** svetlana foote (b). **99 Dorling Kindersley:** Jerry Young (crb). **100-101 Dorling Kindersley:** David Peart (c).

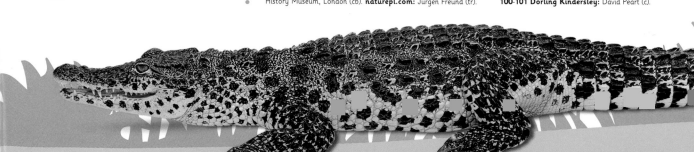

101 123RF.com: Kjersti Jorgensen (br). **102-103 123RF.com:** odmeyer (background). **102 123RF.com:** Eric Isselee (r). **103 123RF.com:** Oxana Brigadirova / Iarus (br). **104-105 Dreamstime.com:** Amwu (c). **105 123RF.com:** Susan Richey-Schmitz (tr). **106-107 Alamy Stock Photo:** Matthijs Kuijpers (b). **106 123RF.com:** Sarayuth Nutteepratoom (cl). **naturepl.com:** Chris Mattison (tr). **107 123RF.com:** Sirichai Raksue (tr); Fedor Selivanov (br). **Alamy Stock Photo:** Chris Mattison (c). **110 123RF.com:** Pedro Campos (bl). **111 123RF.com:** Brandon Alms (cr); weltreisendertj (c); iferol (tc); Dirk Ercken (br); Dirk Ercken (cra); Dirk Ercken (crb); Benoit Daoust (br/ Miniature from). **112 123RF.com:** Vera Kuttelvaserova Stuchelova (b). **iStockphoto.com:** Lumiphil (cra). **113 123RF.com:** ekaterinabaikal (cra). **Dorling Kindersley:** Igor Siwanowicz (crb). **114 Alamy Stock Photo:** Nature Production (cl). **naturepl.com:** Nature Production (cl). **115 Alamy Stock Photo:** Nature Picture Library (tr); tbkmedia.de (cl). **116 123RF.com:** Jens Brggemann (clb); Yavor Yanakiev (crb). **117 123RF.com:** Subrata Chakraborty (cl); Irina Tischenko (cr). **Alamy Stock Photo:** Scott Camazine (cb). **118 FLPA:** Chien Lee / Minden Pictures (cl). **119 Dorling Kindersley. naturepl.com:** Nick Garbutt (bc). **120 123RF.com:** Oleksii Troianskyi (c). **Alamy Stock Photo:** David Liittschwager / National Geographic Creative (br). **120-121 123RF.com:** Shouhei Fukuda (c). **121 123RF.com:** Oleksii Troianskyi (bl). **naturepl.com:** Nature Production (br). **122 Dorling Kindersley:** Jerry Young (clb). **123 123RF.com:** jhvephotos. **124-125 123RF.com:** Alexander Ludwig. **124 Alamy Stock Photo:** Imagebroker. **125 123RF.com:** Mr. Smith Chetanachan (crb). **Dorling Kindersley:** Blackpool Zoo. **iStockphoto.com:** wckiw (bl). **127 Alamy Stock Photo:** Blickwinkel (bc). **naturepl.com:** MYN / Andrew Snyder (cra). **128 123RF.com:** Toby Gibson (clb). **Dorling Kindersley:** Linda Pitkin (cra). **129 123RF.com:** planctonvideo (br); pr2is (c). **Alamy Stock Photo:** Elisabeth Coelfen Food Photography (bl). **130 123RF.com:** Sirirat Chinkulphithak (cra); Eric Isselee (b). **131 123RF.com:** yarlander (cla). **Getty Images:** Ken Usami (b). **132 Alamy Stock Photo:** Jose B. Ruiz / Nature Picture Library (cra). **132-133 Alamy Stock Photo:** Stephen Frink Collection. **133 Dreamstime.com:** Fred Goldstein (crb). **134 Dorling Kindersley:** Andrew Beckett (Illustration Ltd.) (crb); Natural History Museum, London (b). **135 iStockphoto.com:** Hajakely (c). **136-137 Dreamstime.com:** DAJ Digital Archive Japan; Frans Lanting Studio (b). **136 Alamy Stock Photo:** Frans Lanting Studio (bl). **137 Alamy Stock Photo:** Robertharding (br). **138 123RF.com:** Jozsef Szasz-Fabian (clb). **Dreamstime.com:** Fiona Ayerst (cr). **Fotolia:** uwimages (bc). **139 123RF.com:** Maurizio Giovanni Bersanelli (clb). **Dreamstime.com:** Jamiegodson; Picstudio (crb). **142 123RF.com:** aniramphoto (clb); Alberto Loyo (cl); Anastasy Yarmolovich (br). **naturepl.com:** Gerrit Vyn (cr). **143 123RF.com:** Micha Klootwijk (c); Seubsai Koonsawat (cr). **Alamy Stock Photo:** Wild Wonders of Europe / Lundgren / Nature Picture Library (tl). **naturepl.com:** Nature Production (bc). **144-145 Dorling Kindersley:** Oxford Scientific Films. **144 123RF.com:** Michael Lane (cl). **145 Dreamstime.com:** Miroslav Hlavko (cr). **147 Dorling Kindersley:** Judd Patterson (cl); Jerry Young (cla). **148 Dorling Kindersley:** Judd Patterson (tc). **150 123RF.com:** Alta Oosthuizen (cr). **Alamy Stock Photo:** Auscape International Pty Ltd. (crb); Minden Pictures (cr). **151 123RF.com:** Alberto Loyo (tr). **Alamy Stock Photo:** WaterFrame (clb). **152 123RF.com:** josefpittner (l). **Alamy Stock Photo:** blickwinkel (crb). **naturepl.com:** Sandesh Kadur (clb); Konrad Wothe (cra). **153 Dorling Kindersley. iStockphoto.com:** FotoSpeedy. **naturepl.com:** Erlend Haarberg

(clb); Loic Poidevin (crb). **154 123RF.com:** Krzysztof Wiktor (cla); wrangel (clb). **Alamy Stock Photo:** RGB Ventures / SuperStock (clb). **154-155 123RF.com:** Richard Whitcombe (b). **155 123RF.com:** Joseph Quinn (crb); Suwat Sirivutcharungchit (clb). **157 Alamy Stock Photo:** Bruce MacQueen (cr). **158 Dorling Kindersley:** Jerry Young (c). **159 Dorling Kindersley:** Natural History Museum, London (tc); Jan Van Der Voort (b). **naturepl.com:** Daniel Heuclin (c). **160 123RF.com:** Eric Isselee (ca); Anan Kaewkhammul (clb). **naturepl.com:** Brent Stephenson (cb). **161 123RF.com:** Matthijs Kuijpers (clb/Jerboa); Ondrej Prosický (fcr); Vladimir Seliverstov (cla); leisuretime70 (bc). **Dorling Kindersley:** Jerry Young (br). **iStockphoto.com:** Hajakely (c). **162 123RF.com:** Jean-Edouard Rozey (clb). **Dreamstime.com:** Piboon Srimak (crb). **163 123RF.com:** Simon Eeman (clb); Colin Moore (tl). **Alamy Stock Photo:** Alex Mustard / Nature Picture Library (tr). **FLPA:** Jurgen & Christine Sohns (crb). **165 Dorling Kindersley:** Natural History Museum, London (clb). **166-167 Dorling Kindersley:** Andrew Beckett (Illustration Ltd.) (b). **166 123RF.com:** Gleb TV (cla); Zdenek Maly (cl); Phattarapon Pernmalai (cb). **Dorling Kindersley:** Jerry Young (cla). **167 123RF.com:** nrey (c); Phattarapon Pernmalai (r). **Dorling Kindersley:** Andrew Beckett (Illustration Ltd.) (br); Natural History Museum, London (bl). **naturepl.com:** Chris Mattison (tr). **168 Dorling Kindersley:** Rebecca Dean (c); Oxford Museum of Natural History (crb). **Dreamstime.com:** Isselee (cla, ca). **169 Alamy Stock Photo:** Chronicle (t, clb). **Dreamstime.com:** Isselee (cla, ca). **170 123RF.com:** Kostic Dusan (b). **Fotolia:** Norman Pogson (crb). **171 123RF.com:** fedorkondratenko (br); Eric Isselee / isselee (bl). **172 123RF.com:** cylonphoto (clb); Uladzik Kryhin (tl). **Alamy Stock Photo:** Blickwinkel (crb). **173 123RF.com:** Mikkel Bigandt (crb); Phuong Nguyen Duy (clb); Manfred Thürig. **175 Dorling Kindersley:** Jerry Young (tr). **176 123RF.com:** Dirk Ercken (cr). **178 123RF.com:** Marianne Oliva (cr). **Dorling Kindersley:** Gary Ombler (crb). **Fotolia:** Jan Will (cl). **naturepl.com:** Pete Oxford (cra). **179 123RF.com:** 123RFPremium (ca); Eric Isselee (cra); Mr. Suchat Tepruang (cla). **180 123RF.com:** Tim Hester / timhester (c); Keith Levit / keithlevit (cb). **Fotolia:** Photomic (cla). **181 123RF.com:** Bonzami Emmanuelle / cynoclub (cra). **Dorling Kindersley:** Twan Leenders (c); Natural History Museum, London (cb); Jerry Young (clb). **Fotolia:** uwimages (bc). **182 123RF.com:** Oceanfishing (cla). **183 Corbis:** image100 (tr). **Dorling Kindersley:** Blackpool Zoo (br). **184 123RF.com:** Olga Grezova (cra); Anton Starikov (tr); Oleksandr Lytvynenko (cb); Matyas Rehak (cr). **185 123RF.com:** Martin Jose Frade (bc); Saksit Srisuksai (tl); Zarviiolar (c); Rudmer Zwerver (cb); Michael Lane (crb); Beth Partin (bl); Eric Isselee (br); yanukit (cla). **Dreamstime.com:** Michal Candrak (tr); Johncarnemolla (cra). **186 123RF.com:** Hiran Kanthatham (cb); 123RF Premium (cra). **187 123RF.com:** Ishtygashev (tl); Vladimir Seliverstov (ca); leksele (tr); Oxana Lebedeva (fcra). **Dorling Kindersley:** Andrew Beckett (Illustration Ltd.) (cla). **188 Dorling Kindersley:** Hanne and Jens Eriksen (cr); Judd Patterson (cra); The National Birds of Prey Centre (crb). **189 123RF.com:** Ostill (tr). **Dorling Kindersley:** Hanne and Jens Eriksen (cra). **190 123RF.com:** Eric Isselee (cra); Mari art (clb). **191 123RF.com:** Iakov Filimonov (tc); Steve Grodin (cra). **192 123RF.com:** Michaela Dvoráková (cra); Anek Suwannaphoom (crb). **Dreamstime.com:** Vladimir Blinov (c). **193 123RF.com:** Yotrak Butda (tl); Vadym Soloviov (clb); Anan Punyod (cra); Kjersti Jorgensen (crb). **Alamy Stock Photo:** Nature Picture Library (tc). **Dorling Kindersley:** British Wildlife Centre, Surrey, UK (clb). **194 123RF.com:** Eric Issele (cb); Michael Lane (br). **Dorling Kindersley:** Cotswold Wildlife Park

(cla). **195 123RF.com:** Acceptphoto (cl); Michael Lane (c); Renald Bourque (cra); Daniel Prudek (br). **Dreamstime.com:** Nico Smit / EcoSna (tl). **196 123RF.com:** Anan Kaewkhammul (cl); Tom Tietz (cla); Sirylok (cl). **197 123RF.com:** Marigranula (clb); Alta Oosthuizen (c). **198 123RF.com:** Eric Isselee (bl); Kajornyo (tc); Szefei (l/backdrop); Eduardo A Wibowo (cr). **Dorling Kindersley:** Andrew Beckett (Illustration Ltd.) (c). **199 123RF.com:** Anan Kaewkhammul (c). **Dorling Kindersley:** Andrew Beckett (Illustration Ltd.) (cb); Blackpool Zoo, Lancashire, UK (crb). **200 123RF.com:** cla78 (t/backdrop). **Dorling Kindersley:** Jerry Young (cl). **201 123RF.com:** Lynn Bystrom (cla); Eric Isselee (crb). **Dorling Kindersley:** E. J. Peiker (tr). **202 123RF.com:** Isabelle Khn (bl). **Dorling Kindersley:** Linda Pitkin (cb). **202-203 123RF.com:** Mihtiander. **203 Dorling Kindersley:** Linda Pitkin (br). **204 123RF.com:** Vasiliy Vishnevskiy / ornitolog82 (ca). **Dorling Kindersley:** Andrew Beckett (Illustration Ltd.) (c). **204-205 Dorling Kindersley:** Barnabas Kindersley (t). **205 123RF.com:** Andreanita (ca); Dmytro Pylypenko (cra); Konstantin Kalishko (cl); Dmytro Pylypenko (clb). **Dorling Kindersley:** Andrew Beckett (Illustration Ltd.) (cla). **206 Fotolia:** Eric Isselee (c). **207 123RF.com:** Bonzami Emmanuelle (cr); Eric Isselee (cla); Hramovnick (t); Petr Vanek (cl). **208 123RF.com:** Duncan Noakes (cra). **Dorling Kindersley:** Jerry Young (ca). **iStockphoto.com:** Nicholas_Dale (tr). **208-209 123RF.com:** Alexandra Giese (t). **209 123RF.com:** Bennymarty (cl); Eric Isselee (ca); Alta Oosthuizen (c). **Fotolia:** Star Jumper (r). **210 Dorling Kindersley:** Peter Minister (bl). **210-211 Dreamstime.com:** Ollirg (background). **212 123RF.com:** Dmitry Kalinovsky / kadmy (tr). **215 123RF.com:** Eric Isselee (b). **216 123RF.com:** Derek Audette (crb); Jukree Boonprasit (ca); Andrey Gudkov (clb); Ostill (fcra). **217 123RF.com:** Brian Kinney (cr); Thomas Samantzis (tc); mhgallery (cra); Tatiana Thomson (c); Magdalena Paluchowska (cra); Igor Korionov (cb); Juan Gil Raga (cra); Vilainecrevette (bl). **219 Fotolia:** Eric Isselee (tc). **220 Dreamstime.com:** Eric Isselee (bc/tiger body). Photolibrary: Digital Vision / Martin Harvey (bc). **221 Dorling Kindersley:** Natural History Museum, London (bl). **224 Dreamstime.com:** Miroslav Hlavko (br)

Cover images: Front: Dorling Kindersley: Natural History Museum, London crb, Jerry Young cla; **Photolibrary:** Digital Vision / Martin Harvey cb

All other images © **Dorling Kindersley**
For further information see: www.dkimages.com

DK would like to thank:
Martin Copeland, Claire Cordier, Rob Nunn, Surya Sankash Sarangi, Jayati Sood, and Romaine Werblow for picture library assistance, and Marie Lorimer for indexing.